Portraits

Portraits

of Some Bahá'í Women

by

O.Z. Whitehead

George Ronald
Oxford

GEORGE RONALD, Publisher
46 High Street, Kidlington, Oxford OX5 2DN

British Library in Cataloguing Data

A catalogue record for this book is available
from the British Library

ISBN 0-85398-403-4

Typesetting by ComputerCraft, Knoxville, Tennessee, USA
Printed in Great Britain By Redwood Books Ltd.

Contents

*To all those who yearn
for the Truth*

Preface

In the late 1960s Hand of the Cause A.Q. Faizi encouraged me to write about the lives of the early Bahá'ís of the West. I had limited access to information but soon discovered the wealth of material that exists in Bahá'í magazines such as *Star of the West* and *Bahá'í News*, as well as in the yearbook *Baha'i World*. I found it fascinating and valuable to learn about the early believers and to read the Tablets addressed to them by 'Abdu'l-Bahá. Each one of these believers had a unique experience of the Faith: some met 'Abdu'l-Bahá while on pilgrimage to the Holy Land, others met Him during His journeys to the West, still others met Shoghi Effendi or had personal correspondence with him. The life of each of these believers was touched in some way by the power of the Cause and each was transformed. Learning about the lives of these Bahá'ís, I found, has, in turn, a transforming effect on us.

The present book is composed of seven essays about women who chose to use their fine capacities to serve what they loved best in the world, the Cause of Bahá'u'lláh. 'Abdu'l-Bahá Himself has pointed to the important role that women have played in establishing and promoting the Bahá'í Faith in the West: 'Among the miracles which distinguish this sacred Dispensation is this, that women have evinced a greater boldness than men when enlisted in the ranks of the Faith', and 'In this day the duty of everyone, whether man or woman is to teach the Cause. In America, the women have outdone the men in this regard and have taken the lead in this field. They strive harder in guiding the peoples of the world, and their endeavors are greater. They are confirmed by divine bestowals and blessings.'

vii

The seven women here portrayed are examples of 'Abdu'l-Bahá's assertions. Certainly different in personality, expressing their love and service in varied ways, these women, in their unique fashions, fulfilled the wish of 'Abdu'l-Bahá:

For you I desire spiritual distinction; that is, you must become eminent and distinguished in morals. In the love of God you must become distinguished from all else. You must become distinguished for loving humanity, for unity and accord, for love and justice. In brief, you must become distinguished in all the virtues of the human world – for faithfulness and sincerity, for justice and fidelity, for firmness and steadfastness, for philanthropic deeds and service to the human world, for love toward every human being, for unity and accord with all people, for removing prejudices and promoting international peace. Finally, you must become distinguished for heavenly illumination and for acquiring the bestowals of God. I desire this distinction for you. This must be the point of distinction among you.

O.Z. Whitehead
Dublin, February 1996

1

Emogene Hoagg

John Drew, the maternal ancestor of the Bahá'í pioneer Henrietta Emogene Hoagg, migrated from England to the American colonies in 1620 on the Mayflower. Emogene's grandfather, George Zacharias Hodges, and his wife, Eliza, not content with their comfortable life in Boston, moved to the then frontier state of Virginia where George became a colonel in the southern army. In 1848, during the California gold rush, Emogene's father, Dr Martin, made the long sea voyage to the West coast where he married Maria Frances Hodges. They settled in the small mining town of Copperopolis where Emogene was born on 27 September 1869.[1]

Emogene's father died when she was very young. After her mother's remarriage Emogene went to live with an aunt and uncle, Mr and Mrs William Henry Wright, in San Francisco. At 18 she entered Irving Institute, a select boarding school for young ladies, where she studied voice and languages.[2]

Although her parents did not belong to a church – unusual in those days – as a child Emogene had strong religious beliefs. Deciding to join the Congregationalists rather than the Catholics, the only two churches in Copperopolis, she attended services regularly and accompanied the hymns on the piano.

As she grew older and sat through the long sermons every Sunday morning, Emogene asked herself, 'Why did the good God of all men love only Christians?' Since He had created not only Christians but all others too, she could find no logical answer to this question. Although she did not stop

1

going to church, her faith was shaken by doubts and she gradually thought of herself as an agnostic.[3]

At the age of 20 Emogene married John Ketchie Hoagg, the son of a New York Dutchman. John was a successful engineer who 'had made a fortune in flour mills'.[4] They had no children and, after several years of marriage, John permitted Emogene, accompanied by a family friend, to travel to Milan to study voice. She stayed for over a year. By the time she returned home in 1898, at the age of 29, Emogene had still not found the answer to her religious questions. Soon afterwards she made what turned out to be a very important visit.

Emogene visited the famous philanthropist Mrs Phoebe Apperson Hearst at her home in Pleasanton, California. Here she met Lua Moore Getsinger, 'the mother teacher of the West', and her husband, Dr Edward Getsinger. Mrs Getsinger was teaching her hostess the Bahá'í Faith.

Even without tangible proof one can readily believe that the Cause of God provided the main subject of conversation during Emogene's visit. According to Amine De Mille, in whose home Emogene lived for nine months at the end of her life, when the Getsingers first spoke to Emogene about the coming of Bahá'u'lláh, she immediately became interested. Through their analysis of His writings the Getsingers were able to dispel all of the doubts and misconceptions about religion that had greatly disturbed Emogene since her early teens.[5] Ella Goodall Cooper wrote of this, 'Emogene was so attracted by Mrs Getsinger's earnest manner that she sought for daily lessons with her, resulting in Emogene's instant acceptance of the Faith.' Emogene herself affirmed, 'My interest augmented from lesson to lesson. The first commune, "O my God, give me knowledge, faith and love", was constantly on my lips, and I believe those words from the Fountain of Eternal Light awakened my soul and mind to a faith that has never wavered.' As a result of the meeting at Mrs Hearst's 'Hacienda' Emogene became the first confirmed believer in California.[6]

In December 1892, with 'Abdu'l-Bahá's approval, a Syrian doctor, Ibráhím George K͟hayru'lláh, who was a gifted Bahá'í teacher, travelled from Egypt to the United States. In February 1894 he moved from New York City to Chicago, where he began to teach the Cause with extraordinary success.

On hearing that this dynamic speaker and magnetic personality had attracted many seekers, Emogene travelled from California to Chicago so that she might attend Dr K͟hayru'lláh's lectures.

Unfortunately, by this time K͟hayru'lláh had deviated from Bahá'u'lláh's teachings. The doctrine of reincarnation was then very popular, particularly among the Theosophists who attended K͟hayru'lláh's classes. Hoping to make Bahá'ís of them, he incorporated their doctrines into his lectures, even calling 'Abdu'l-Bahá the reincarnation of Christ. He included this theory in his book *Bab-ed-Din* (The Door of True Religion).

Deeply affected by all that she had heard about the Bahá'í Faith, Mrs Hearst arranged to visit 'Abdu'l-Bahá in the Holy Land in 1898. Among the 14 guests whom she generously invited to accompany her on this unforgettable pilgrimage were Dr K͟hayru'lláh and his wife. Accepting Mrs Hearst's invitation, K͟hayru'lláh decided to show his book to 'Abdu'l-Bahá in the hope of persuading Him to approve it. However, 'Abdu'l-Bahá not only rejected the book but instructed K͟hayru'lláh to discontinue his teaching. As a result of his egotism and ambition, K͟hayru'lláh turned away from the Faith. Through the power of his personality and the cleverness of his intellectual arguments, he was, unfortunately, able to influence several others to do the same.

Emogene, however, like other strong Bahá'ís who formed the nucleus of the future American Bahá'í community, remained unshaken in her belief. She later told Mrs De Mille that Mrs K͟hayru'lláh had written to her from 'Akká, saying, 'Forget everything that you have been taught except that Bahá'u'lláh came and has passed away. 'Abdu'l-Bahá, the Centre of the Covenant is here, but He is not the reincarnation of Jesus Christ.'[7]

In the midst of the confusion that followed <u>Kh</u>ayru'lláh's defection, Emogene found it a relief to return to Milan. Here she received her first Tablet from 'Abdu'l-Bahá, penned in response to her letter accepting the Faith written from California. Shortly afterwards Emogene moved to Paris to find another voice teacher. In Paris the much loved young American May Ellis Bolles had established the first Bahá'í centre in the continent of Europe. Emogene had the uplifting experience of getting to know all of its members. This little community was a 'haven of peace and unity after America'.[8]

In November 1900 and with the Master's permission, Emogene, accompanied by her friends Helen Cole and Alma Albertson, set sail for Haifa. At that time 'Abdu'l-Bahá and His family were living in the House of 'Abdu'lláh Pá<u>sh</u>á in 'Akká. When the three pilgrims arrived in Haifa, the Master's trusted servant, Isfandiyar, drove them directly to the Tomb of Bahá'u'lláh in a carriage drawn by three horses. At this most holy spot Bahíyyih <u>Kh</u>ánum, the eldest daughter of Bahá'u'lláh and known as the Greatest Holy Leaf, and Díyá <u>Kh</u>ánum, the eldest daughter of 'Abdu'l-Bahá, gave them a warm welcome.

Later that day the Master greeted them with great love at the door of His house. Emogene's bedroom in this house 'was decorated with utmost simplicity. Its only furnishing was a cot. Here, she slept for ten nights in perfect comfort . . .' The Master met with Emogene and her two travelling companions every day, 'instructing them in the divine Message bequeathed to a dying civilization by His Father'.[9] According to Ella Goodall Cooper, Emogene's pilgrimage was her 'spiritual baptism'.[10]

Shortly before the end of her stay, the Master suggested to Emogene that she should spend some time in Port Said to study the Bahá'í interpretation of the Bible with the greatly revered scholar Mírzá Abu'l-Faḍl. Such was 'Abdu'l-Bahá's opinion of him that He often requested Abu'l-Faḍl to instruct individuals and the infant communities of the West. Emogene has written:

For four weeks Mírzá Abu'l-Faḍl received me at the home of Núr'u'lláh Effendi twice a day, morning and evening, and gave me such explicit instruction on the Bible that for the first time this Book became an open page. It was not without difficulty that I got the explanation. Sometimes Núr'u'lláh Effendi would give me the meaning in Italian, and at other times Aḥmad Yazdi Effendi would translate into French. Then I would put their words into English. After about two weeks Anton Haddad was sent to Port Sa'íd and he translated directly into English. Almost every evening five or six of the Bahá'í brothers would meet with us to hear Mírzá Abu'l-Faḍl's explanations. Those were wonderful days . . .[11]

According to Mrs De Mille, 'These lessons set the pattern for all her future service to the Faith. She became henceforth a student of the Holy Scriptures, not only of the Bahá'í and Judeo-Christian Dispensations, but also of the other world religions so little known in the West at that time.'[12]

As a result of her intensive study with Mírzá Abu'l-Faḍl, Emogene thought of composing a comprehensive compilation which she entitled 'Three Worlds' and later 'The Three Conditions of Existence: Service, Prophethood and Deity'. Although she laboured hard on this monumental work off and on for many years, and often used it in her teaching efforts, she did not complete it until shortly before her death.

In February 1901 Emogene travelled from Port Said to Paris. Although she greatly enjoyed being with the Bahá'ís there once again, she soon became anxious to see her family and to describe to the believers in America her imperishable experiences in the Holy Land. Much to her delight Emogene found that she and Lua Getsinger were sailing on the same ship for home. During a most happy voyage together the two ladies spoke about the coming of Bahá'u'lláh to many people.

On her arrival in New York City, Emogene learned that the Master had sent Mírzá Abu'l-Faḍl to America so that he might dispel the doubts which the defection of Dr

Khayru'lláh had engendered in the hearts of some of the believers and to increase the understanding of the community. At the time he was teaching at Green Acre, in Eliot, Maine, which Sarah Farmer had formally opened in 1894 in order to help bring about the unity of humankind. Before travelling across the continent Emogene and her friend Helen Cole spent some time at Green Acre and again had the privilege of studying with Mírzá Abu'l-Faḍl.

In 1902 'Abdu'l-Bahá revealed for Emogene a precious Tablet which, according to Mrs Cooper, Emogene always carried with her. Anton Haddad translated it:

> O thou who art rejoiced at the Glad Tidings of God!
>
> I received thy last letter in which thou showest thy wistful consent to the good pleasure of God, thy resignation to His Will and thy evanescence in the way of His wish.
>
> O maid-servant of God! I assuredly know thy spiritual feelings, thy merciful thoughts, thy firmness in the Cause of God, thy straightforwardness in the Testament of God.
>
> It is incumbent upon thee to have good patience and to endure every grave and difficult matter. Patience is one of the gifts of God, an attribute of the elect, and a mark of the righteous.
>
> I supplicate God to bestow upon thee a power and a blessing to enable thee to guide sincere servants and devoted maidservants to enter the Garden of El-Abhá. This is better unto thee than that which is in existence in this world of creation. This is a fact!
>
> Be tranquil because of My love to thee and My prayers for thee, and rejoice at all times and under all circumstances.
>
> O maid-servant of God! How excellent is that sentence thou hast written in thy letter: 'It behooveth me to eliminate self (or egotism) so that I will not desire anything but the Will of God.' How good is this prayer, and how beautiful is this invocation. Aught else besides this makes it impossible for man to be confirmed by the abundance of the gift of God; neither will he succeed in becoming a humble and submissive servant or a labourer in His Great Vineyard.
>
> My salutation and praise be upon thee![13]

On her return to San Francisco in January 1903 Emogene found that Helen Goodall and her daughter Ella Cooper were occasionally holding Bahá'í meetings at their home in Oakland and had already attracted a small group of people to the Faith. Emogene now helped her two friends establish regular weekly firesides. When late in 1907 Mrs Goodall and Ella left Oakland to go on pilgrimage to 'Akká, Emogene held the meetings in her own home so that the teaching would not be interrupted during their absence of several months and even added a second weekly meeting for deeper study. Amine De Mille has related:

> Teaching during those first years was slow. It was generally felt that meetings should be made very sacred, so the Faith would not become one of the 'isms' flowering profusely in America at the turn of the century. The Message was spread guardedly by word of mouth. Publicity was considered worldly and even dangerous. The fanatical and prejudiced shunned the Bahá'ís, refusing to contemplate such revolutionary, even sacrilegious ideas, and associate with these socially unacceptable people. Although in the Western Hemisphere the believers were not physically harmed, nor was their property pillaged and confiscated as in the East, yet they endured, as 'Abdu'l-Bahá had predicted, a mental and emotional torture and a social ostracism.[14]

In June 1903 the Chicago Bahá'ís received a Tablet from 'Abdu'l-Bahá in which He gave His most enthusiastic approval to their request for His permission to build a House of Worship in America. The Master's further encouragement and contributions from a few communities decided the Chicago Bahá'ís to invite representatives from various parts of the country to meet in Chicago on 26 November 1907 at the home of Mrs Corinne True in order to initiate the proposed project. Bahá'ís from nine communities attended this historic meeting and appointed a committee of nine to select a suitable site for the Temple.[15]

Since Mrs Goodall was by then on her way to 'Akká, Emogene took her place as the representative from California. Mrs True recorded, 'Emogene's flaming spirit of devotion was one of the pioneer pillars who accomplished that great step in the progress of the Faith in this country.'[16]

On the unforgettable morning of 11 April 1912 'Abdu'l-Bahá and His attendants arrived from Alexandria via Naples in the harbour of New York City on the steamship *Cedric*. This was the beginning of a journey of untold importance to the progress of the Bahá'í Faith, a journey which in a period of eight months was to take 'Abdu'l-Bahá across the North American continent.

From 25 July to 16 August the Master and His entourage stayed in the attractive village of Dublin, New Hampshire. During this time Emogene and Mrs Cline, also of San Francisco, resided at the Dublin Inn as the guests of Mrs Agnes Parsons and her husband, Arthur. According to Joseph Hannen, another guest at the Inn, as soon as he and the other Bahá'ís had settled themselves comfortably, 'Abdu'l-Bahá came to see them and a delightful meeting took place. 'Abdu'l-Bahá spoke of His travels:

> See how much we have moved from one place to another. How far New York is from here: Washington, Chicago, Philadelphia, the many places we have visited.

Then, referring to Emogene and Mrs Cline, He said,

> And now these ladies have come to invite me to come to California. They are supplicating that I should come to California. Now these two have come to insist that we shall go; and letters are coming about it. A letter came yesterday from the Spiritual Assembly, asking how it came that we went to other places and not there. Now Mrs Hoagg is going to build an aeroplane and take me there. What do you advise? Shall I ride on it?

Mrs Hannen replied, 'It would not be very safe.' 'Abdu'l-Bahá responded with a smile, 'When I ride on it, it is the Ark of Noah. This aeroplane will become the Ark of Noah.'[17]

From Dublin Emogene followed the Master to Green

Acre, remaining for the entire week of His visit. Later, 'Abdu'l-Bahá did visit California for nearly four weeks in October 1912, travelling to San Francisco, Oakland, Palo Alto, Berkeley, Pasadena, Los Angeles and Sacramento. While He was there Emogene did everything she could for Him, calling herself His 'bell boy'.[18]

On 5 December 1912 'Abdu'l-Bahá and His attendants sailed from New York City on the S. S. *Celtic* to Liverpool. At the end of His second visit to the British Isles, on 21 January 1913, He left for Europe, remaining there until the following June. On 13 June He sailed from Marseilles for Port Said where He landed four days later. Shortly after His arrival He became feverish and on 17 July He moved to Ramlih, a suburb of Alexandria, where it was thought the weather was more salubrious.[19]

As soon as Emogene heard that the Master was in the Middle East she wrote for permission to join Him. By the time she received it, she was confined to bed with a severe illness. Even so, she insisted on leaving immediately. Since her husband would not permit her to travel alone, she invited a friend to accompany her.

When Emogene arrived in Ramlih she was still weak and ill. She asked 'Abdu'l-Bahá for a remedy. 'He sent her two baked apples, with instructions to eat them at once. She did; seeds and all. She then went to bed and slept soundly. The next morning she was quite well.'[20]

As a result of His strenuous travels in Europe and North America the Master was tired and run down. In an effort to regain His physical strength before returning to His home in Haifa, where a large amount of work lay before Him, He stayed in Egypt for four and a half months. It appears He had little rest:

> . . . pilgrims arrived constantly and had to be accommo-
> dated and entertained. He was never alone or free from
> demands. He could never refuse one who came to Him for
> whatever purpose.[21]

When in early November 1913, partly in response to pleas from His own family, the Master decided to return home, He sent Emogene and two or three other pilgrims ahead to prepare for His return. In a letter to the American friends dated 27 December 1913 Emogene wrote of His arrival:

The home coming of Abdul-Baha, after an absence of three years and four months, was a real festival. Such excitement and happiness as reigned in the holy household can only be imagined . . . In Abdul-Baha's house, there is a very large central room around which are the other rooms, and in it Persian rugs were spread and tables placed upon which were fruits and sweets . . .

When Abdul-Baha's voice was heard as he entered, the moment was intense – and as he passed through to his room, all heads were bowed. In a few moments he returned to welcome all. He sat in a chair at one end of the room, and most of the believers sat on the floor. Abdul-Baha was tired so remained but a short time, and after a prayer chanted by his daughter Zia Khanum, went to his room.

Then the ladies vacated so that the men might enter. To see the faces of those sturdy, earnest men – faces that spoke the fervor of their faith, the earnestness and resoluteness of their purpose – was something to remember . . . He welcomed them, and seating himself on the floor, spoke to them a short time, after which he retired . . . There were old tried veterans, whose lives have been devoted to the Cause, and courageous, aspiring youths . . .

Abdul-Baha seems to feel best at Acca. He left here the second day after his arrival, remained eight days, then came to Haifa for a week and is again at Acca.[22]

During her pilgrimage Emogene sent a letter to the American Bahá'ís quoting the words of 'Abdu'l-Bahá's wife, Munírih Khánum:

Baha'o'llah, when he was six years old, had a dream in which he saw himself swimming in a mighty ocean which was so great that he marveled. His hair, which was long, was floating out on the waves and soon he discovered that to each separate hair a fish was attached by its mouth, that is, the fish was holding the hair in its mouth. There were large fish, small fish, white fish, black fish, in fact all kinds of fishes. The impression he received was so vivid that he was awakened. When he told his father in the morning the father decided to have the meaning if possible. Being, as you know, a Grand Vizier, he applied to the Shah, asking permission to have the dream interpreted by the court interpreter of dreams. This was granted him. When the interpreter had heard the dream he stood amazed. He said, 'This is a most wonderful dream, but I do not see how it can come true. The ocean symbolizes the world; the fish are the people of the world who are to gain knowledge from this boy – knowledge of God. You must protect and keep him, for he will be very great, but it is not possible that he can fulfill entirely such a wonderful dream. How can the entire world receive knowledge of God from this boy? However, this is what I see in this dream. Protect him. Keep him and guard him. He will be very great and teach great and learned people as well as others.'[23]

Emogene remained in the Holy Household for nine months. In July 1914 'Abdu'l-Bahá sent her to London with Munírih Khánum's brother to warn the English believers that Dr Amínu'lláh Faríd, Munírih Khánum's nephew, had disobeyed 'Abdu'l-Bahá and was now cut off from the Faith. During 'Abdu'l-Bahá's American tour he had caused the Master much concern and great sorrow, acting in a generally erratic and destructive manner as well as secretly soliciting money from some of the rich believers. Now he was travelling in Europe and was planning to become a leader of the Faith in London.[24]

Emogene was still in London in August 1914 when the first world war broke out. Unable to return to the continent, she joined other Bahá'í women working for the Red Cross until December, when on the advice of the American-born Mary Virginia Thornburgh-Cropper, the first Bahá'í in the British Isles, she joined Lady Blomfield in Paris to work at the American hospital. Emogene stayed only briefly in Paris, travelling once again to Milan, this time to help in the war work. Nervous strain and poor food caused her health to deteriorate and she returned to her home in San Francisco, where she lived until her husband's passing in 1918.

In the spring of 1917 Emogene attended the ninth annual national convention of the Bahá'í Temple Unity at the Hotel Brunswick in Boston. In March 1909, 39 delegates representing 36 cities had attended a conference in Chicago to establish a permanent national organization to oversee the building of the House of Worship on the shores of Lake Michigan. The Bahá'í Temple Unity was created and an Executive Board of nine elected to serve it. Emogene was elected to the Executive Board at the 1917 convention, along with Albert Hall, Corinne True, Alfred Lunt, William Randall, Roy Wilhelm, Agnes Parsons, Eshte'al-Ebn Kalantar and Harlan Ober.[25]

From 10 to 12 November 1917 the Chicago 'House of Spirituality' held a celebration of the hundredth anniversary of the birth of Bahá'u'lláh. Emogene, who chaired the session in which the illustrious Dr Zia Bagdadi spoke of the conference as 'the first convention for teaching', read to those assembled the Tablet revealed by 'Abdu'l-Bahá on 29 March 1916 for the central states of America.[26] In one passage 'Abdu'l-Bahá assured the believers:

> . . . I am engaged in writing you this brief epistle so that my heart and soul may obtain joy and fragrance through the remembrance of the friends. Continually this wanderer supplicates and entreats at the threshold of His Holiness the One and begs assistance, bounty and heavenly confirmations in behalf of the believers. You are always in my thought. You are not nor shall you ever be forgotten. I hope by the favour of His Holiness the Almighty that day by day you may add to your faith, assurance, firmness and steadfastness, and become instruments for the promotion of the holy fragrances.[27]

This Tablet was the third in a series of fourteen that the

Master revealed to His American followers over the course of a year, the first eight between 26 March and 22 April 1916 and the remainder between 2 February and 8 March 1917. Entitled the *Tablets of the Divine Plan*, these letters honoured the American believers by giving to them a world mission which would take many years to fulfil. Five of these Tablets, all providing instructions on teaching the Bahá'í Faith in the North American continent and in the islands off Canada, appeared in the Bahá'í magazine *Star of the West* of 8 September 1916. The rest could not be dispatched until the end of the war and they were first unveiled at ceremonies during the 'Convention of the Covenant' – the eleventh annual national convention and Bahá'í congress – held in April 1919 in New York.[28] These Tablets called upon the Bahá'ís to spread the Cause of God throughout the planet.

The convention opened with a reception in the Congress Hall of the Hotel McAlpin. As a member of the Executive Board of the Bahá'í Temple Unity and of the National Reception Committee, Emogene was among those who welcomed the delegates and guests.[29]

In the Tablet revealed on 8 April 1916, 'Abdu'l-Bahá wrote, referring to Margaret Duncan Green:

> Alaska is a vast country; although one of the maid-servants of the Merciful has hastened to those parts, serving as a librarian in the Public Library, and according to her ability is not failing in teaching the Cause, yet the call of the Kingdom of God is not yet raised through that spacious territory.[30]

'Abdu'l-Bahá mentioned Alaska again in His Tablet of 8 March 1917 in which He listed a large number of countries and territories requiring Bahá'í teachers:

> Therefore, O ye believers of God in the United States and Canada! Select ye important personages, or else they by themselves, becoming severed from rest and composure of the world, may arise and travel throughout Alaska . . .[31]

As soon as Emogene read these Tablets she was filled with a strong desire to travel to Alaska.[32] She received a cable from 'Abdu'l-Bahá approving the journey and, together with Marion Jack, set off for the 'vast country'.

Marion Elizabeth Jack, whom Shoghi Effendi called an 'immortal heroine',[33] was born in Saint John, New Brunswick on 1 December 1866 into a prominent family. She first learned of the Bahá'í Faith through Charles Mason Remey at a dance while a student in Paris around the turn of the century. Shortly afterwards Marion dedicated her life to the Bahá'í Cause.[34]

Emogene and Marion sailed from San Francisco to Alaska on the steamship *Victoria* in July 1919. They travelled first to Nome, arriving about 15 July, and then to St Michael, where they arrived on 24 July. From there they travelled up the Yukon on the *Julia B*, a commercial boat that stopped at a number of communities along the way.[35] Amine De Mille relates:

> Sometimes, the little steamer made only one mile an hour, but everywhere they pulled up, even for a few minutes, the two women would hop ashore and leave pamphlets with as many people as they could speak to. If the stop were long enough, they would go into the shops, visit the hotels and lodge halls, the movie theatres and restaurants. At Tenana, a Chinese restaurant owner became so enthusiastic that he began passing our pamphlets to all his customers, saying, 'This is very good! You read! Do you a lot of good!'[36]

Emogene noted in her diary that the villages they passed in the boat were picturesque if not 'extraordinary in architecture'.[37] Marion often set up her easel on the street and did some sketching. After a few people had gathered she would turn to them with a winning smile and say, 'Did you ever hear of the Bahá'í Cause?' If they seemed interested she would wave them towards Emogene, saying, 'Go over and talk to Mrs Hoagg, she can tell you all about it!'[38]

The two women travelled to Dawson, where they stayed

with some distant relatives of Marion. Here they received letters from 'Abdu'l-Bahá's family, letters Emogene called 'gifts from the Holy Presence'.[39]

From Dawson Emogene and Marion travelled to Whitehorse and then took the train to Skagway. Here their teaching efforts met with some resistance. Although at first they could not understand why this was so, they soon discovered that previous visitors there had said that Bahá'ís advocate 'free love'.[40]

The two women travelled next to Juneau, where Marion stayed while Emogene took the boat to Cordova, Valdez, Seward and Anchorage. At Cordova she wrote in her diary, 'While I gave only one public talk, the whole town was astir with the Message . . . It really rejoices one to know that the hearts are being prepared so opportunely, and that all we have to do is to lend our services.'[41]

Concerning her experiences in Anchorage Emogene wrote, 'Some of the women at Anchorage helped to arrange talks . . . They thought it was wonderful to travel and teach without taking pay, and that it was a privilege to hear the addresses. I stand in awe at the power of the Spirit that will provide these means and opportunities.'[42]

Emogene returned to Juneau on 21 December. During the Christmas holidays she and Marion had a series of dinner and teaching engagements in private houses. On New Year's Eve they attended a reception given by Governor and Mrs Riggs. Late that evening Georgia Greyson Ralston arrived from New York to accompany Emogene on trips to towns near Juneau.[43] They made fleeting visits to Sitka, Wrangell and Ketchikan.

Their visit to Sitka coincided with the Greek holidays and they could not rent a hall owing to all the dances taking place. When Georgia wondered what they would do, Emogene replied, 'Well, if we cannot get a hall on account of a masked ball, we will go to the ball. There we are sure to see everyone, and some may be willing to listen to us.' Their attendance at the ball produced good results: they interested a number of people in the Bahá'í Faith.[44]

Emogene wrote from Wrangell to a friend in Washington DC on 15 January 1920:

> One must adapt the way to the needs, and the main thing is to have the people learn about the Faith . . . I know I shall miss the pioneer spirit of Alaska. I certainly like it here.[45]

Emogene and Georgia began their journey home from Juneau, sailing from Vancouver to San Francisco on 24 February. Emogene recorded in her diary her mixed feelings about her sojourn in Alaska. All Alaska, she wrote, had heard the call of 'Yá Bahá'u'l-Abhá' but no new believers had come forward.[46]

Home again, Emogene attended, as a delegate from Berkeley, California, the twelfth annual conference of the Bahá'í Temple Unity, held in New York in April 1920. In his comprehensive report of the event, Alfred Lunt related:

> The Convention entered into consultation concerning the best means of assisting the newly appointed national teaching committee. The question of literature for distribution at such meetings was brought up and the crying need of this manifested. Mrs Hoagg spoke on this subject and suggested that if each of the friends would donate one dollar a month to the teaching fund it would be of the utmost assistance.[47]

Late in the spring of 1920 Emogene made her third pilgrimage to the Holy Land, where she remained for six months as the guest of 'Abdu'l-Bahá. At His request she looked after the pilgrims: when, for example, Genevieve Coy arrived with Mabel Paine, Mabel's daughter Sylvia (later Mrs Parmelee) and Cora Grey on the first of September, it was Emogene who met them at the door of the pilgrim house and settled them into their rooms.[48] Genevieve recalled a conversation with Emogene in the Master's garden:

> I shall not forget the look on Mrs Hoagg's face when she spoke of the Master's longing for unity among the friends. His only happiness is to know the increase of unity among

the believers, and of their spreading the Cause. His face always becomes sad if he hears of any contention or lack of harmony. 'If people in America could see the Master, could realize how he works, they would never do anything to sadden him,' she said. When one is in the Master's presence it seems utterly impossible that one should ever do anything that would sadden, or make any heavier the load of work he carries! 'In the light of his holy presence, all desire dies save the desire to be like him.'[49]

According to Mrs De Mille, one day the Master sent for Emogene and asked her what she thought of the North American Bahá'í community. After she had described some of her experiences and made some observations about them, she asked Him why there was not more unity among the American Bahá'ís. In reply 'Abdu'l-Bahá told her a story of a man who went to his doctor for treatment. Every complaint the man made about this pain and that was met by the doctor's comment, 'That is due to old age.' When the man became angry and asked the doctor how it was that he had nothing more to say to a patient than that his illness was due to old age, the doctor relied, 'Your anger, too, is due to old age.' Then the Master rose from His seat, said, 'The condition in America is due to lack of steadfastness,' and left the room.[50]

Early in November 1920 'Abdu'l-Bahá said to Emogene that He wanted her to leave for Naples as a pioneer. Emogene obeyed at once. She knew no one in Italy but, after several lonely months, owing to a suggestion made by a mutual friend, an invitation arrived from Signora Borghese for Emogene to give a Bahá'í talk at her palace in Rome. About 20 guests attended.

As Emogene was leaving the palace a count stopped her and thanked her for her talk, expressing his admiration for her courage in giving it. He asked her how she had been able to get into 'this black (meaning Roman Catholic) stronghold'. A few days later he called on Emogene and asked her to give a lecture at his mother's home.

The count's mother greeted Emogene when she arrived but did not stay. The audience consisted of a large group of men, most of whom were socialists who showed a definite interest in what Emogene said. As a result of this talk, one of the guests gave her the address of General Piola Caselli in Naples. He in turn arranged for her to speak at the home of his sister, Signora Orlando, where 25 to 30 people listened to Emogene's talk.

Thus over a short period Emogene was able to give the Bahá'í message 'to three widely different strata of Italian society: the old Catholic aristocracy, the modern intellectuals with army connections, and social-idealists'.[51]

Soon afterwards Emogene was invited to speak at a centre for university students in Naples. From among these students she succeeded in establishing a weekly study class at her hotel. She was also able to teach the Faith in Milan and Torino where a few people became Bahá'ís.

Shortly after one o'clock in the morning of 28 November at His home in Haifa, 'Abdu'l-Bahá ascended to the Kingdom of Abhá. Later that day, while she was in Torino, Emogene received from His sister Bahíyyih Khánum, the Greatest Holy Leaf, a cablegram informing her of this heartbreaking event. As soon as Emogene obtained permission to do so, she left Italy for Haifa. She later told Mrs De Mille:

> It was terrible to go to Haifa and not see 'Abdu'l-Bahá there. He had been the law that pervaded every decision, every act of family and friends. His daily habits were the pattern around which their lives were woven. It was everyone's love for Him that made this possible, and kept the routine on its orbit.[52]

Although for a week Emogene could not think properly, after that she was much occupied helping to translate some important Tablets. In one of them, the last He revealed for the Bahá'ís of America, 'Abdu'l-Bahá warned the believers to beware of those who sought to destroy the Covenant of Bahá'u'lláh. The translation made by 'Mrs Hoagg, Ali

Mohemmed Bakir and Rouhi after His passing' read in part:

> In America, in these days, severe winds have surrounded the
> lamp of the Covenant, hoping that this brilliant light may
> be extinguished and this Tree of Life may be uprooted.
> Certain weak, capricious, malicious and ignorant souls have
> been shaken by the earthquake of hatred, of animosity, have
> striven to efface the divine Covenant and Testament, and
> render the clear water muddy so that in it they might fish.
> They have arisen against the Centre of the Covenant like
> the people of the *Beyan* who attacked the Blessed Beauty
> and every moment uttered a calumny. Every day they seek
> a pretext and secretly arouse doubts, so that the Covenant
> of Baha'Ullah may be completely annihilated in America.[53]

Unavoidably delayed, Shoghi Effendi, his sister and Lady
Blomfield arrived in Haifa from London on 29 December.
Although he was 'weak and ill with grief, he restored order
and purpose' to the situation.[54]

Forty days after the Ascension of 'Abdu'l-Bahá, on 7
January 1922, His Will and Testament was publicly read at
His home in Haifa. Emogene related to Mrs De Mille that
at least a hundred Bahá'í men from various countries attended this unforgettable event. Five or six American and
English women, including Emogene, sat among them in the
central hall. The oriental women, she recalls, sat in a side
room 'out of sight, but near enough to hear'.[55] As 'Abdu'l-
Bahá's secretary read the Will, many people wept. Its impact
was tremendous. The Master had placed emphasis on the
untold suffering caused by the Covenant-breakers.

'All present accepted the terms of the Will appointing
Shoghi Effendi Guardian. There seemed to be no dissenting
voice.'[56]

On 24 January Emogene wrote to Corinne True:

> Before long the Will (and Testament) of the dear Master will
> be ready for America and elsewhere. Shoghi Effendi is
> translating it now. How wonderfully the Beloved provided
> for the protection of the Cause. This will be a happiness to

the sincere and a test to the weak. Let us pray that the friends in America will arise with strength and goodwill to obey and to serve. This is the least we can do now, that the beloved Master may be pleased with us, and forgive our many omissions as well as commissions . . .[57]

In February Shoghi Effendi called together a group of well-known Bahá'ís, including Emogene, to consult with him on matters concerning the future development of the Faith, particularly whether the Universal House of Justice should immediately be established. Afterwards, the Guardian decided that he could not possibly call for the election of the House of Justice until local and national assemblies were functioning in those countries where Bahá'í communities existed.

Emogene remained in Haifa for as long as she thought the Guardian needed her. Then she and Munavvar Khánum, one of the Master's daughters, left for Germany. After they had made visits to Swartzveld, Frankfurt, Berlin and Stuttgart, Emogene returned to Italy where she knew 'Abdu'l-Bahá wanted her to teach. Establishing herself in Rome, she began to hold regular meetings for students.

Early in 1923 Emogene moved to Florence, where she remained for three years. In the attractive garden of her house she entertained guests and taught them the Faith. Although most of those she taught were deaf to the call of the Cause, one Signora Campini became a devoted believer and co-worker. Signora Campini helped translate into Italian *The Wisdom of 'Abdu'l-Bahá* and John Esslemont's classic textbook *Bahá'u'lláh and the New Era*.

In 1925 Mrs Jean Stannard, encouraged by the Guardian, established the International Bahá'í Bureau in Geneva as 'a centre designed primarily to facilitate the expansion of the teaching activities of the Faith in the European continent'.[58] In its pleasantly furnished rooms Mrs Stannard, Martha Root and Lady Blomfield, as well as outside speakers, addressed audiences and entertained guests. Bahá'ís visiting Geneva found the Bureau a most suitable centre in which to meet and visit one another. Owing to the careful planning and determination of Martha Root, the Esperanto Society held its annual Congresses here in 1925 and 1926.[59]

In July 1926 Mrs Stannard published the first of four issues of *Messager Bahá'í*, printed in English, French and German. Shoghi Effendi was delighted with the magazine and urged her to bring out further editions. In 1927 her failing health prompted her to ask Julia Culver to assist her. In the autumn of 1927 Mrs Stannard's health and financial situation made it imperative that she leave Geneva at once. Julia took over the entire responsibility for running the centre, providing as well most of its financial support.

In May 1928 Julia wrote to the Guardian explaining that she needed help and suggesting that Emogene be invited to work with her. The Guardian was pleased with this suggestion and in June Emogene left Florence for Geneva.

According to Shirley Warde, Julia and Emogene assembled a library, initiated a bulletin published between 1927 and 1935 and arranged lectures and social events to bring people of like interests together. Under their direction the Bureau 'cooperated with all organizations in Geneva that were striving towards goals similar to those of the Bahá'ís, maintained contact with the activities of the Faith throughout the world' and made it 'an auxiliary nerve centre to Haifa'.[60]

In 1931 Shoghi Effendi invited Emogene to Haifa to assist him in the typing and preparation of the manuscript of an epic history of the early days of the Bahá'í Cause that he had recently translated from Persian into English. Composed by Nabíl, a contemporary of the Báb and Bahá'u'lláh, the Guardian gave the work the exciting title *The Dawn-Breakers*.

On completing this important and stimulating task Emogene returned to Geneva. When in 1934 a scarcity of funds made it necessary to move the Bureau to smaller premises and to curtail its activities, Emogene thought the moment had come for her to leave. The Guardian agreed and encouraged her to return to America where she was needed to deepen the believers, particularly in the Administrative Order.

From her arrival in the United States early in 1935 until late 1940, Emogene, under the direction of the National Teaching Committee, travelled throughout a large part of the country, including a visit to Montreal. In 1937 she attended Green Acre and made fine use of an outline prepared by her that 'covered the fundamental subjects of the Faith' in the five morning sessions she led on the *Dispensation of Bahá'u'lláh*.[61] The April 1938 edition of the *Bahá'í News* that reported this also recorded that Emogene 'spent some time in Southampton, Long Island, and gave a series of six Public Forum Discussions to which the entire Southampton Colony was invited'. The Southampton Bahá'ís took out an eighth of a page advertisement in three of the local papers, each with a circulation of about 3,500. When this series of meetings was completed, Emogene conducted a study class at the home of Mrs John Anderson.[62]

The November 1938 *Bahá'í News* carried an announcement that 'Conditions of Existence: Servitude, Prophethood, Deity', a study outline compiled by Mrs H. Emogene Hoagg, originally published under the title 'Three Worlds', was on sale for 50 cents a copy.[63]

Established in 1931, the Louhelen Bahá'í School is situated at Louhelen Ranch near Davison, Michigan. Beginning on 1 May 1938, before the summer sessions had begun, Emogene conducted a study class two evenings a week in the nearby Flint community and gave talks to a number of groups in towns not far away.[64] From the 9th to the 19th of the following July the Summer School Committee directed a Laboratory Session designed to prepare individuals for the teaching field.[65] Emogene gave one of the four courses; using her outline, she emphasized the 'need for a more exact presentation of the Bahá'í Teachings'.[66]

In her introduction to this scholarly outline, Emogene explained:

In the 'Three Worlds' or three planes of being as given in the Bahá'í Teachings we find clearly defined the relationship of all creation to God, the Essence, the Unknowable, the Source, and its direct dependance upon the Manifestations of God's Essence.

When studied diligently we are able to understand the vital difference between the teachings of the mystics, of some of the philosophers, of many of the present-day cults, and the concepts as given by the revealed words of the Manifestations pertaining to this relationship.

From this understanding of the 'Three Worlds' we shall be freed from any and all ideas regarding immediate nearness to the Essence of God and be able to grasp the meaning of that Unity that is the fundamental life-force penetrating . . . all creation.

From it we shall also escape the prevalent general tendency to personify the absolute in the Manifestation to such a degree that the Unknown Essence, the Source is forgotten.

On the other hand we are to realize that the distinct place of the Prophets – that Primal Emanation from the Absolute – is our only approach or medium to that Absolute, the great 'Central Light'.

We become aware of the true significances: I) of the Oneness of God in His essence; II) of the Oneness of the Manifestations with that Source; III) of the essential Oneness of the Manifestations in relation to each other; and IV) of the oneness of humanity in its reality . . .

Thus we realize that these three planes of being are distinct in their reality, but indissolubly linked by the one Source that binds together and penetrates all existence.[67]

The Laboratory Session at Louhelen School was so successful in the summer of 1938 that the committee decided to repeat it the next summer. A notice appearing in the *Bahá'í News* of May 1939 directed: 'Those attending the Laboratory Session are asked to bring, if they can, *Some Answered Questions, Bahá'í Scriptures, Gleanings, Promulgation of Universal Peace, Foundations of World Unity, Hidden Words*, and Mrs Hoagg's outline entitled "Conditions of Existence: Servitude,

Prophethood, Deity". Also to please study in advance pages 6 through 9 of this outline.'[68]

Emogene's outline consists of seven sections: World of God, World of Command, World of Creation, Bahá'u'lláh, the Báb, 'Abdu'l-Bahá and the Administrative Order. All contain a large number of brief references to the holy writings on subjects relevant to the section title.

'World of Creation', four pages of which the friends were requested to study before coming to the Laboratory Session, consists of 24 parts, each with a sub-title. Among the many quotations of Bahá'u'lláh cited by Emogene is 'God's creation hath existed from eternity'.[69] She then points to other passages in the Bahá'í writings in which Bahá'u'lláh has amplified this subject.

Emogene suggested that her outline could be used for both individual and group study as well as a source for topics for articles and quotations for Nineteen Day Feasts and devotional meetings.

In 1940, at the age of 73, Emogene accepted an assignment from the Inter-American Teaching Committee to make a visit of some months to Cuba, for which she taught herself Spanish. Eugenio Ginés, the first believer in Cuba, relates that Phillip Marangella and his wife Laili had brought the Faith to the country the previous year.[70] When Emogene arrived in November, a month after the Marangellas had to return to the United States, she found a group of earnest believers in Havana, all of whom had much affection for the Marangellas.[71]

Laying particular emphasis on the Administration, Emogene tried to deepen the group in its understanding of the Cause. When in the ensuing January Miss Josephine Kruka joined her, the two held Bahá'í classes twice a week and started to teach the believers English. Emogene gave a public address at the Woman's Club of Havana; an article about her lecture appeared in the *Havana Post*. By the time Emogene left Cuba in April 1941, two new believers had joined the Havana community.[72]

On her return from Cuba Emogene suffered a heart attack while visiting in California. She never fully recovered. Even so, when in 1943 she heard that one more Bahá'í was needed in Greenville, South Carolina, to form an Assembly, she somehow managed to get there.

In May 1944 Emogene was able to attend, at the House of Worship in Wilmette, Illinois, the thirty-sixth annual convention of the Bahá'ís of the United States and Canada and the Bahá'í Centenary celebration commemorating the hundredth anniversary of the founding of the Bahá'í Faith.

In her vivid 'Impression of the Centenary', the distinguished Bahá'í writer Marzieh Gail has related, 'Mrs Emogene Hoagg, California's first Bahá'í, read from 'Abdu'l-Bahá's words on the power of the Covenant; Emogene Hoagg, not at all bowed down by her years of endless service – among the most notable being her typing of the *Dawn-Breakers* at the Guardian's direction.'[73]

In September 1944 Emogene moved to Washington DC where for several weeks she remained as a guest of Miss Leone Barnitz before going to the home of Amine De Mille in Chevy Chase, Maryland, for nine months.

Although Emogene was confined to bed for almost all of this time, she occasionally found it possible to get up and conduct a deepening class for a few believers. When, as often happened, she became very ill, Mrs De Mille 'would cable the Guardian for prayers as was the custom in those days, and she would seem to improve. Then, pale and thin, her blue eyes glowing, she would ask for her writing material and books. Propped up on pillows, surrounded by a mountain of books, she would write on her manuscript . . .'[74]

During this time Emogene's brief but scholarly essay on the three volumes of *Tablets of 'Abdu'l-Bahá* appeared in the *World Order* magazine of June 1945. In her clear and forceful explanation of the enormous importance of these Tablets, which with a few exceptions were addressed to American believers, she affirmed:

To the early believers they were the greatest source of joy and enlightenment – enlightenment relative to the spiritual and material problems of daily life as well as those of deeper significance. As there were no English translations of the Writings of Bahá'u'lláh, these early Tablets were the avenue through which the understanding of the New Revelation was most clearly conveyed to the Western world . . . Each Tablet received was eagerly shared with the friends; the translation immediately copied, and sent to individuals in the different centres . . . As the Faith spread the number of Tablets arriving spread accordingly.[75]

In July 1945 Mrs de Mille was saddened to learn that she could no longer give Emogene the care that she needed. Adeline and Carl Lohse drove her to Charleston, South Carolina, where she was looked after for the last five months of her life by Josephine Pinson. Miss Pinson wrote a touching account of Emogene's death:

> About eight days before she passed, she had a very bad heart attack, and she said then that she knew the end was near. She asked for a pencil and pad and wrote out the following message to be cabled to the Guardian immediately after her passing: 'Last loving greetings, Emogene'.
> After that, she spoke very little of going, but grew weaker each day.
> The joy with which she announced her departure cannot be described in words . . .
> 'Come Josie, quick! I am going!' She wore an expression of supreme happiness, which she kept until the end. There was a light in her eyes which seemed to envelop her entire face, and all the marks of age seemed to disappear. She lived on for more than an hour after that . . .
> Then she called to me in a joyous mood, extended her hand and took mine, 'Goodbye, I'm gone!'
> She passed away in heavenly ecstasy at 9:30 o'clock on the evening of December 15, 1945.[76]

On hearing the news of Emogene's death, the Guardian cabled to the National Spiritual Assembly of the United States and Canada:

Deeply grieved passing staunch exemplary pioneer Faith, Emogene Hoagg. Record national, international services unforgettable. Reward Abhá Kingdom assured, abundant.[77]

Emogene's body was buried near her last home, in Magnolia Cemetery in Charleston.[78]

2

Claudia Coles

Claudia Coles was born Claudia Stuart Smith in Charleston, South Carolina, in 1863.[79] Four years later she experienced a double tragedy. Her mother, who was pregnant, was fatally injured while trying to save the life of a girl whose clothes had caught fire. Shortly afterwards Claudia's father died as a result of wounds he received in the American Civil War. Claudia thus found herself alone with her younger brother Frank. They went to live with different relatives, Claudia with an aunt in Philadelphia.

Claudia was a lovely child and grew up to be a beautiful girl. A brilliant student with many interests, she particularly excelled in photography.[80]

In 1887 Claudia married Tucker Coles of Albemarle County, Virginia. He had a fine character, was well-liked and came from a rich and prominent family. Two years later Claudia gave birth to a daughter, whom they named after his sister, Lelia Skipworth. Soon afterwards, Mrs Skipworth, who was living with her husband in an attractive house on her magnificent estate, Enniscorthy, suggested to Tucker that he manage Coleswood, the large sugar plantation in South Carolina that they jointly owned. Thinking well of the idea, Tucker followed his sister's proposal.

Although not physically strong and suffering from diabetes, Tucker worked very hard on the plantation, travelling around it each day on horseback. More and more concerned about the gradual decline of her husband's health, Claudia complained to her sister-in-law that he was over-taxing himself and asked her to take some responsibility for the running of the plantation. Mrs Skipworth was not pleased with Claudia's remarks and a certain coolness developed between them. Claudia felt that her sister-in-law was being very unjust to Tucker and could not understand her attitude. Tucker himself did not complain, however, and continued to work as hard as ever.

One day in 1892, on her return from a short visit, Claudia found Tucker in a deep coma. After a brief but painful illness he died. Broken hearted, Claudia moved with her daughter Lelia back to Virginia. While Lelia was growing up they divided their time between Virginia and California. Although Lelia was named in her aunt's will as the heir to Enniscorthy, an unscrupulous lawyer who was also a distant relation succeeded in erasing her name from the document. Lelia later took her case to court but was unsuccessful, falling ill during the hearing.[81]

While Claudia was visiting Washington DC, probably early in 1905 although the exact date is not known, she first met Mariam Haney. This remarkable and courageous lady had been a Bahá'í for about five years and she soon convinced Claudia that Bahá'u'lláh had revealed the word of God for this day. Soon afterwards Claudia established her residence in Washington with Lelia and took a job as a secretary in the Pentagon building. Judging by a charming photograph of Claudia taken at the time, she had a beautiful face, lovely eyes and a warm, gentle but firm expression.

To a Tablet revealed for the distinguished Bahá'í Hooper Harris in 1905, the Master added a message for Claudia: 'Express to her my greetings of affection, my warm greetings, and say "Sow the seeds! The sun and rain are very good. This is the outer law; and be certain that God causes things to grow." I am the witness of this, be sure, be certain.'[82]

On 14 November 1906 Claudia received her first Tablet from the Master. It began with these lines:

O thou loving God! Guide thou this supplicating servant to the station of sacrifice, make her to become firm and steadfast in this most great cause.[83]

Less than a month later M. Ahmad Esphahani translated a second Tablet revealed by 'Abdu'l-Bahá for Claudia:

> O thou dear maid-servant of God! Thank thou God that thou hast been created in the Days of the Manifestation on the Mount of Sinai; hast attained to faith and assurance; beheld the light of truth; hast been delivered from the darkness of heedlessness and hast become endowed with the powers of knowing, seeing, learning and speech. Know thou the value of this gift, and render praise to His Highness the Merciful One. Upon thee be Bahá-El-Abhá![84]

In another Tablet revealed for an unnamed believer, translated on 16 February 1907, the Master advised Claudia:

> The end of every material work is without result, because it is perishable and inconstant, but the first real work is attraction to the fragrances of God, enkindlement with the fire of the love of God, reading the verses of unity and beholding the lights from the Dawning-place of Mystery. After that comes the training of souls, purification of character and service to humanity. If thou art able to accomplish any one of these, the result is eternal and the fruits everlasting.[85]

'Abdu'l-Bahá revealed another Tablet for Claudia on 21 June 1907:

> Truly I say, thou art patient and thankful and art firm and steadfast amidst the tests, like unto an unshakable mountain. The proof of it is this, that thou didst not become despondent on account of the illness of thy daughter, neither didst thou lament and grieve. Thou didst resign thy will to the will of God and became satisfied with the Heavenly decree.[86]

In the *Bahá'í News* (later called *Star of the West*) of 21 March 1910, the first edition of the magazine, Claudia's name is listed as one of the 12 members, all women, of the recently established Unity Band. Each member had the task of writing monthly to one of the twelve Women's Assemblies in Iran. Claudia was assigned to write to 'Esphahan' (Isfahan). 'Abdu'l-Bahá had been most pleased with the results of the work of the Unity Band in the previous year and 'in a letter received by one of the members from Mirza Aziolah Khan, of Teheran . . . he assures her of the great joy and happiness these letters bring to these dear sisters of the East, and earnestly begs their continuance'.[87]

In obedience to the instructions of 'Abdu'l-Bahá, the Bahá'í community of North America held its first general convention at the Masonic Temple in Chicago on 22 and 23 March 1909. The 39 delegates assembled first established a permanent national organization, the Bahá'í Temple Unity, and elected an Executive Board of nine members to direct the building of the first House of Worship in the Western world.

A little more than a year later, on the morning of 24 April 1910, at this same location, as a prelude to the second Bahá'í Temple Unity convention, a moving festival service took place. Claudia, along with other notable Bahá'í speakers, gave a short talk during the service. At the convention itself Claudia was appointed to the auditing committee whose seven members had the job of finding ways and means to start to erect the Temple; she was also appointed to a committee of three charged with the task of composing a letter of gratitude to the friends in the orient for their great services to the Cause.[88]

Principally for the purpose of arousing interest in and gaining support for the Tarbiat School for Boys in Iran, a Persian-American Educational Society was founded in Washington DC. 'Abdu'l-Bahá declared that this society could do much to unify East and West and Bahá'ís were encouraged to join. 'Abdu'l-Bahá revealed several Tablets about the Tarbiat School. In one He wrote:

The problem of the School of Tarbiat is of the utmost importance. It is an essential obligation and duty incumbent upon all the friends to serve that school. This is the first school that the friends have founded in Persia, and all the people know that its belongs to them . . . It is the hope of this Servant that in the course of time this school become distinguished from among all the schools of the world.[89]

Claudia was the librarian of the Persian-American Educational Society and requested through the *Bahai News* that literature for the school, both books and magazines, be sent. Her address was given as 310 The Burlington, Washington DC.[90]

The 4 November 1910 edition of the *Bahai News* carried an appealing if somewhat indistinct photograph of the first 30 children to receive their education at the Tarbiat School owing to contributions made by members of the Persian-American Educational Society. The list of benefactors gives Claudia and Louis Gregory as providers of a scholarship for 'Abol Gasem'.[91]

As a fitting prelude to the third Bahá'í Temple Unity convention on Saturday evening, 29 April 1911, the Spiritual Assembly of Chicago held a Feast of Unity at 125 North Wabash Avenue. During the formal part of the feast, Joseph Hannen read to the friends a Tablet recently revealed by the Master which He wished them to hear without delay. It read in part:

Now the friends and the maid-servants in America have written innumerable letters and all of them are pleading that Abdul-Baha make a trip to that country. Their supplications and entreaties are insistent. In view of the differences among the friends and the lack of unity among the maid-servants of the Merciful, how can Abdul-Baha hasten to those parts? Is this possible? No, by God!

If the friends and the maid-servants of the Merciful long for the visit of Abdul-Baha, they must immediately remove from their midst differences of opinion and be engaged in the practice of infinite love and unity . . . Verily, verily I say

33

unto you, were it not for this difference amongst you, the inhabitants of America in all those regions would have, by now, been attracted to the Kingdom of God, and would have constituted themselves your helpers and assisters.[92]

During the conference Claudia and other believers gave in succession short talks on the need for love and unity among all the friends. According to Mr Hannen, Claudia's speech 'thrilled with ringing utterances'.[93]

On the next afternoon, despite inclement weather, nearly 50 of the friends, including Claudia, travelled from Chicago to Wilmette to visit the site of the proposed House of Worship.

At the morning session of the second day of the convention, a committee composed of Joseph Hannen, Homer Harper and Claudia which had been appointed to investigate the purchase of additional grounds at the Temple site made its report. On a motion made by Claudia and duly seconded, the convention voted to authorize the Executive Board of the Bahá'í Temple Unity to proceed with the recommendation in the report to purchase six further plots.[94]

At the public meeting that closed the convention that evening Claudia gave an introductory talk on the Bahá'í Faith entitled 'The Message' in a 'spacious hall filled with delegates, friends and visitors'.[95]

Late in the summer of 1911 Claudia travelled to London to meet 'Abdu'l-Bahá. She was among those who greeted Him in the hall of Lady Blomfield's house at 97 Cadogan Gardens when He arrived there at the start of His first visit to England on 8 September. According to His hostess, these believers 'arrived eager and elated nearly every day during His sojourn, often bringing a friend or relation'.[96] Claudia's granddaughter Claudia Kelly described the meetings of her grandmother with the Master as the 'culmination of her life'.[97]

While Claudia was still in London she received a Tablet from the Master:

O thou who art enkindled by the fire of the love of God! Verily, I have perused thy beautiful letter of wonderful composition, which proveth thy firmness, assurance and steadfastness in the faith . . . Know that the building of the Mashrak-el-Azkar is the greatest foundation in those regions . . . It is incumbent upon thee and upon all, to put forth the best effort in these days, in building this glorious Temple . . . It is incumbent upon ye (men and women) to be united, in this great Cause, so that ye may be confirmed by the Divine Bounty, and Merciful Spirit; become increased with energy and power; gain a recompense, and estimation. I implore God, and supplicate Him to make your feet firm in the straight path, and in the upright way.[98]

Claudia's comments on this Tablet appeared in the *Star of the West*:

Abdul-Baha expects to attend the Convention to be held in Chicago during the coming spring-time. Unquestionably, he will dedicate the site of the Mashrak-el-Azkar at that time.

Through the guidance of God this site has been chosen, and Abdul-Baha's wish that there be room for ample grounds is being obeyed . . . if in selflessness, humility and unity we serve together in earnest effort – his desires will be fulfilled and the site of the Mashrak-el-Azkar (The Dawning Place of the mentioning of God) found ready for his consecration.[99]

The Master did come to the United States the following year and attended the national convention. At the Feast of Riḍván preceding the convention, on the Saturday evening 27 April, Claudia, among many others, presented greetings to the delegates and friends.[100]

Three evenings later, on Tuesday 30 April a public meeting to end the convention was held in Drill Hall Masonic Temple. 'The announcement that Abdul-Baha would be present constituted a fitting climax to a wonderful series of sessions', wrote Joseph Hannen of the event.[101] Upon His entrance into the hall, the more than one thousand people who crowded into the hall arose as one and maintained a 'breathless silence' as He proceeded to the platform. The Master then gave a most moving and persuasive talk explaining the great importance of building the first House of Worship of the Western world. At one point He said:

The world of existence may be likened to this temple and place of worship. For just as the external world is a place where the people of all races and colours, varying faiths, denominations and conditions come together – just as they are submerged in the same sea of divine favours – so, likewise, all may meet under the dome of the Mashriqu'l-Adhkar and adore the one God in the same spirit of truth; for the ages of darkness have passed away, and the century of light has come.[102]

The next morning the friends assembled in a tent erected near the centre of the Temple site and waited for the Master to appear. Honore Jaxon reported that 'the majesty and simplicity of his mien as he briskly advanced on foot toward the tent – a far spread line of the friends forming an escort just behind him – constituted a scene which will be remembered by those who witnessed it as one of the most impressive experiences of their lives'.[103]

When the Master reached the middle of the huge tent, He paced up and down before the assembled guests. About 300 chairs had been set out and another 200 people were standing. He gave a brief but vivid description of what a House of Worship should be like.

At the end of the talk everyone moved out of the tent and gathered around the exact centre of the site. Irene Holmes of New York presented 'Abdu'l-Bahá with a golden trowel to break the earth. Then He called for an axe and shovel to make a place to lay a stone brought by Esther Tobin and chosen by Him to be the cornerstone of the Temple. Those present took the tools in turn to break the ground in the name of every race and nationality represented. 'Abdu'l-

Bahá finally laid the cornerstone on behalf of all the people of the world, then left for Chicago while the friends remained to converse or wander through the grounds.[104]

In 1913 the convention of the Bahá'í Temple Unity was held for the first time outside Chicago. It was held on 28 and 29 April in New York City, named by 'Abdu'l-Bahá the previous year as the City of the Covenant. Claudia had been appointed, together with Alfred Lunt, Roy Wilhelm, Corinne True and Edna McKinney, to a committee to consider ways and means of speedily beginning the work on the Temple. The committee's report to the convention noted that 'the key to this, we believe, is love and solidarity, and the swiftest means is a systematic and regular giving. But love must urge, and our gifts be of the heart, else they fail of consecration.'[105]

Claudia spoke about the future Temple from the convention floor:

> Abdul-Baha has said that the work of the Temple is not a matter of individual effort but of united effort. There is first the spring, then the rill, then a great river and then the mighty ocean. May that be the way in which we work for the Mashrak-el-Azkar.[106]

Claudia's job at the Pentagon earned her only a modest salary. One day, however, a friend gave her a thousand dollars. Mariam Haney relates that Claudia rushed off with it as quickly as she could to Josephine De Lagnel, who was responsible for the Temple funds at that time, and told her to send the whole amount to the Temple straight away.[107]

Although she was not physically strong, Claudia would hurry home from work every afternoon to host the tea-parties to which she invited many people. On these occasions she would 'shine radiantly as a teacher, and would reach exalted heights'.[108]

On Sunday 24 April 1914 Claudia spoke at the public meeting at the sixth annual convention of the Bahá'í Temple Unity. Using quotations from the Bible to support her points, she said that those from a Christian background could increase their understanding of the Bahá'í Faith by a careful study of the Old Testament and Gospels.[109]

Two years later, at the eighth annual convention, Claudia addressed the delegates in these moving words:

> When I first heard of the Mashrak-el-Azkar I prayed to God for prosperity that I might help build this glorious temple. Since then I have walked the way to Damascus. I have seen a new light. I have learned that the way is to pray for the prosperity of the whole world. I pray that this spiritual fire of God's Holy Spirit may go forth over the world, burning away all human ignorance and limitations, that it may burn in us as in the apostles of old until we go forth with such spirituality that the material things vanish before our eyes, and we set men's hearts aflame with the fire which has descended upon us from heaven. Then shall we transmit to the people of our age that spirit of the new birth which shall of a truth build the Temple of the Lord.[110]

The next year Claudia addressed these words to the convention:

> In this day no matter what mistake we make, it can be corrected, because the power of the Holy Spirit is surging through the whole world . . . Our duty is merely to look at the Centre of the Covenant and receive the light that is shining . . .[111]

On 11 November 1917 Claudia spoke at the Centennial Festival of the Birth of Bahá'u'lláh arranged by the Chicago Bahá'ís, an event that was celebrated over three days with 'spiritual joy' and 'heavenly harmony'.[112] Claudia's address, delivered at the Auditorium Hotel, was on the subject of the emancipation of women and universal suffrage. Louis Gregory described her talk:

> She was very well fortified with the Holy Utterances and proved the station of women with spiritual illumination. She had an array of facts, historical and otherwise, which carried conviction. She gratefully acknowledged the bounty of Baha'o'llah which made men and women equal. She be-

lieved that the ideal freedom would come to women through spiritual and educational unfoldment; through evolution rather than a revolution.[113]

Harlan Ober reported on the conduct of the tenth annual convention of the Bahá'í Temple Unity held in April 1918. His report mentions Claudia a number of times. Regarding plans for the erection of the Temple she said:

> I stand here as one of the little group that in the early convention put 95 cents into the building fund. I remember so well how we went to Mrs True and gave her 95 cents, one by one, and put it in her hand with faith, with love, with trust, with confidence and with absolute assurance that the prayer that went with that 95 cents put into Mrs True's hands was the seed planted that would bring about this great growth. And to think that the $200,000 goal is so near, and that we so soon may be able to cable to Abdul-Baha that we have fulfilled his requirements – the thought makes for so much greater dynamic power, that we seem to see that temple built.[114]

Those present applauded Claudia's remarks with enthusiasm.

At this convention Claudia was appointed chairman of a committee to compile the Bahá'í writings on the Most Great Peace. Other members of the committee were 'Mrs Maxwell, Mr Remey, Mrs Cooper, Dr Bagdadi, Mr Vail, Mrs Hoagg, Miss Thompson, Mrs Rabb'. It was agreed that a copy of the completed compilation, together with a letter setting out the Bahá'í principles, would be sent to President Woodrow Wilson and to every head of state whom the committee could reach.[115]

Claudia edited the diary of Major Wellesly Tudor-Pole, which was published in *Star of the West*. In late 1917 Tudor-Pole, who was serving in the Holy Land, heard that 'Abdu'l-Bahá was in great danger of His life. The major did everything he could to ensure the Master's safety. In November 1918, seven days after the First World War ended, he travelled from Jerusalem to Haifa in the hope that he might attain the presence of 'Abdu'l-Bahá. He describes that meeting:

> The Master was standing at the top waiting to greet me with that sweet smile and cheery welcome for which he is famous. For seventy-four long years Abdul-Baha has lived in the midst of tragedy and hardship, yet nothing has robbed or can rob him of his cheery optimism, spiritual insight and keen sense of humour.
>
> He was looking a little older than when I saw him seven years ago, and certainly more vigorous than when in England after the exhausting American trip. His voice is as strong as ever, his step virile, his hair and beard are (if possible) more silver-white than before . . .
>
> After lunch Abdul-Baha drove me out to the Garden Tomb of Baha'o'llah about two miles from the city . . . He approached the Tomb in complete silence, praying with bent head – a wonderfully venerable figure in his white turban and flowing grey robe.
>
> On reaching the portal to the Tomb itself, the Master prostrated himself at length, and kissed the steps leading to the inner chamber. There was a majestic humility about the action that baffles description.[116]

A short time later Claudia received a Tablet from 'Abdu'l-Bahá, translated by Shoghi Effendi on 28 January 1919:

> He is God!
> O thou beloved maid-servant of God!
>
> Thy letter dated October 4, 1918, was received. It was not a letter but rather a bouquet of flowers diffusing the sweet scent of firmness and steadfastness and so it gave pleasure to the nostrils of the soul.
>
> Praise be to God, the test proved to be the cause of the firmness and the steadfastness of the people of faith.
>
> Throughout these years of disturbance and commotion, when the world of humanity was physically and spiritually afflicted, the friends of God passed the day in rest, ease and comfort. In the western countries only a few shared in the hardship and affliction of other souls while the mass of the

friends and the maid-servants of the Merciful, of whom Mrs Coles is one, have been living quietly and peacefully. In the orient every nation became distracted and every gathering dispersed save the friends of God who all remained protected and sheltered from every trouble and calamity in the fort of Baha'o'llah's protection. Verily, this is a divine miracle – that we helpless, friendless, unprotected, unsupported wanderers in these regions should be saved amidst the fire of oppression and tyranny. This is God's miracle.

In fine, praise be to God, yourself and the friends of God and the maid-servants of the Merciful have, like unto an unmovable rock, remained firm and resolute in the Cause of God.

Organize ye meetings and strive day and night that ye may be the cause of the diffusion of divine fragrances and the exaltation of the Word of God.

Concerning the book [*The Mysterious Forces of Civilization*] that thou hadst written about; it has been written on political affairs so that justice and equity may be promoted and the comfort of the world of mankind may be realized.

Upon thee be Baha-el-Abha![117]

Later that year, from 26 April to 1 May, the eleventh convention of the Bahá'í Temple Unity was held at the Hotel McAlpin in New York City. Claudia served on the National Reception Committee at this important event at which the 14 Tablets of the Divine Plan were unveiled. These Tablets, revealed by 'Abdu'l-Bahá in 1916 and 1917, gave the Bahá'ís their spiritual mission.[118]

Late in 1920 Claudia moved to London, where her daughter Lelia Skipworth Aldridge and granddaughter Claudia were already living. As soon as she settled her home became a gathering place for Bahá'ís and enquirers alike. A great many believers from other countries visited her and always received a warm welcome.

The British Bahá'ís had established a Bahá'í Council in 1914 but this had stopped functioning in 1916 when World War One was at its height. On 16 January 1920, a few days before the end of Dr John Esslemont's extended visit to the

Holy Land, the Master asked him to set the Cause aflame in London and to reestablish the Bahá'í Council. As there were only a few believers in England, the Master told him that it would not be necessary to hold an election. As a result of this conversation, the newly formed Council met for the first time in December, at Miss Grand's flat in London. Its 12 members included Ethel Rosenberg, Mary Virginia Thornburgh-Cropper, Annie Gamble, Elizabeth Herrick, Florence 'Mother' George and Eric Hammond from the original council and Helen Grand, Miss Musgrave, Mrs Crosby, George Simpson, Dr Esslemont and Claudia.

'Abdu'l-Bahá had made some corrections to Dr Esslemont's book *Bahá'u'lláh and the New Era* while Esslemont was in the Holy Land. Early in 1923 Shoghi Effendi sent him further suggested revisions and Esslemont consulted both Ethel Rosenberg and Claudia about the corrections.[119] In the introduction to his book Esslemont expressed his gratitude to Claudia 'and many other kind friends for valuable help in preparation of the work'.[120] Claudia Kelly notes that her grandmother undertook extensive research for Dr Esslemont and typed the entire manuscript.[121] The completed book was praised highly by Shoghi Effendi, who called it 'the textbook of the Faith'[122] and said it would 'inspire generations yet unborn'.[123]

Although 'Abdu'l-Bahá had in the spring of 1910 given Claudia permission to come to 'Akká for nine days,[124] she had for some reason been unable to do so. In March 1924, however, Claudia set sail from London to begin her pilgrimage. On 14 March, in Haifa, she met up with her friend Helen Grand, who had travelled from New York. Shoghi Effendi was absent from the Holy Land at the time, which must have been a great disappointment to the two women, but they did have the precious experience of meeting his great aunt Bahíyyih Khánum, the Greatest Holy Leaf. Miss Grand has related:

I shall never forget our first walk through the Master's garden, where He had spent so many hours making it beautiful with every flower one could imagine. The garden is steeped with memories of 'Abdu'l-Bahá and one feels His continued presence, making it truly a Holy Garden, where prayers, night and day, have been offered to God for the brotherhood of the world and the unity of the nations. Every evening we walked upon Mount Carmel to the tomb of 'Abdu'l-Bahá and spent an hour or more in the twilight; the great silence and peace were deeply wonderful.[125]

In the autumn of 1924 the 'Conference on Some Living Religions within the British Empire' was held under the auspices of the School of Oriental Studies and the Sociological Society at the Imperial Institute, South Kensington in London. Shoghi Effendi had hoped to attend but was unable to do so owing to the burden of his work. In his place Mountfort Mills read a powerful paper on the Bahá'í Faith, while Shoghi Effendi's cousin Ruhi Afnan read a second paper on some of the practical applications of the teachings of Bahá'u'lláh.

At this same conference Richard St Barbe Baker, an assistant conservator of forests in Kenya since 1920, presented his paper 'Some African Beliefs concerning the Faith of the A-Kikuyu'. The members of this tribe, he later confirmed, worshipped Mwinyaga, possessor of whiteness, who dwelt in Kirinyaga, 'Place of Whiteness'. They were kind to each other and did not have the word 'devil' in their vocabulary. He concluded his paper by saying, 'To understand them we must go with them into the silence of the forest and learn what for us, as well as for them, is the secret of life, the love the Mwinyaga, the great white spirit.'[126]

Claudia was in the audience. At the end of his talk she approached St Barbe, saying, 'You are a Bahá'í. You are just as interested in the other man's religion as your own.' St Barbe replied, 'This is so.' He introduced Claudia to Mrs Grant-Duff, a close friend of his, then shook hands with the

Bahá'ís and others who crowded around him to thank him for his sympathetic presentation of an African belief. From this time on a close friendship developed between Claudia and St Barbe.[127] Ten days later, just before his departure for Nigeria, Claudia gave St Barbe his first Bahá'í books.

In 1922 St Barbe had established the 'Men of the Trees' among the Kikuyu of Kenya as a way to encourage the young village men of the region to plant trees to replace the lost forests. In 1929 the High Commissioner of Palestine, Sir John Chancellor, asked St Barbe to apply the lessons he had learned in Kenya to the protectorate, which was suffering from the encroaching desert. Chancellor believed that only by securing the agreement of the different religions in Palestine to a collective action could the problem be tackled. St Barbe agreed to undertake the task and approached Shoghi Effendi, who asked to become the first life member of the Men of the Trees. According to St Barbe himself, Claudia was 'one of the most active members of the Council of the Men of the Trees' and was a 'great inspiration' in his life.[128] Almost four years after her passing St Barbe wrote to Martha Root:

> I have had extraordinary success in my work. Looking back I realize how much of my success was through the spirit I caught from Claudia.[129]

In December 1925 *The Bahá'í Magazine* carried a brief but appealing essay by Claudia entitled 'To Make Holy'. It begins:

> How wonderful the inner meaning of the word Sacrifice – '*to make holy*'! True sacrifice, 'Abdu'l-Bahá tells us, 'means joy and giving life to the spirits'! In it is a spiritual transformation, not asceticism nor exclusion of bounty, but the fulfilment of the great purpose in nobleness.
>
> In God's great plan for the life on earth, the progress of mankind is through the sacrifice of ignorance for the growth of knowledge; the sacrifice of envy, hatred, malice, and all uncharitableness, for love, sincerity, and blessed forgiveness.

The essay continues by explaining the sacrifices of the Manifestations of God and calls upon the Bahá'ís to render service to the Cause of God in the spirit of such sacrifice. It ends with this beautiful statement:

> This is the hour of preparation. Now is the Day of sanctification, of purification, of judgement. The Day when imperfection will be sacrificed to become perfection, when those who are born of spirit shall make a willing sacrifice of manmade licence, to the Divine Law; of man-made politics, to Divine Policies; of man-made mistakes, to Divine Guidance; of man-made confusion, to Universal Peace; of man-made sorrow, to Divine Healing; of man-made night through the gloom of the World, to the Day of God, and that Day – *Happy!*[130]

In May 1922 the British believers, acting on the instructions of Shoghi Effendi, elected the first All-England Bahá'í Council, composed of ten Bahá'ís from London, including Claudia, and one Bahá'í each from Bournemouth and Manchester. The first meeting of the Council was held on 17 June at the home of Mrs Thornburgh-Cropper in Westminster, London. The next year this body was dissolved and the first National Spiritual Assembly of the British Isles elected, meeting for the first time on 13 October 1923.

Claudia was elected onto the National Assembly in 1925 and remained a member for the rest of her life, sometimes serving as secretary.

In June 1926 Martha Root arrived in Britain for a five-month stay. In addition to giving talks every day or evening, she wrote two hundred letters to newspapers and societies calling attention to the persecution of the Bahá'ís in Iran, as well as taking care of an enormous correspondence relating to the Esperanto conference to be held in Edinburgh later that summer. Rather critical of Martha when they had met in America some years before, Claudia now realized her mistake and became a close friend. She wrote to Julia Culver, who had paid for secretarial help for Martha:

What a God send you are. There is absolutely nothing that you could have thought of that would be more of a help just now to Martha than to provide her with an expert stenographer and typist.

It will make all her work at Edinburgh and here easier and enable her to do a lot of things that she could not have done . . .

She looked so happy when I gave her your message about getting a stenographer, and felt it such a help . . .

. . . I have said nothing about clothes, but thought when you did come you could get Martha a suit, or Kasha dress to use for speaking &c. later on . . .[131]

During the First World War the London Bahá'ís were unable to hold regular meetings. In 1919 they found that it was again possible to do so and hired Lindsay Hall in Notting Hill Gate. Here they met regularly every Wednesday evening until mid-1929. In that year the National Spiritual Assembly acquired its first permanent Bahá'í Centre at Walmar House in Upper Regent Street in London. The new centre was opened on 19 September:

A large number of the friends were gathered on this occasion to celebrate what is to many of them a direct answer to the prayers that have been offered for the spread of the movement during the past year.[132]

The acquisition 'changed the outlook' of the Bahá'ís:

As a result of nine months' earnest prayer for the advancement of the cause, they saw this room at Walmar House, a permanent home instead of a little room hired for two hours once a week.[133]

In about January 1930 the Guardian wrote to the National Spiritual Assembly through Claudia:

. . . I am delighted with your new centre, and will pray at the Holy Shrines from the depths of my heart for its progress. Kindly assure my dear English friends of my heartfelt appreciation of their staunchness, their renewed activity, their self-sacrificing endeavours. I will continue to pray for their individual, as well as their collective efforts, from the bottom of my heart.[134]

In April 1930 the British Bahá'ís held their first national convention at Walmar House. Claudia was once again elected to the National Spiritual Assembly as its secretary and wrote in the *Bahá'í News*:

> We have entered upon a new year of work with a sense of deep thankfulness for all the blessings of the past year, and of gratitude to God for His unspeakable mercy and love to us. But as we look forward we realize how tremendous are the opportunities and responsibilities lying before us – opportunities which we can never cope with until we obey more consistently the teachings of the Master – responsibilities which we can never adequately fulfil until we avail ourselves of the Mighty Power of the Holy Spirit ever ready for the assistance of every obedient faithful soul.[135]

Never physically strong, during September 1930 Claudia became ill and grew steadily weaker. Although above all else she remained anxious to attend meetings, she found it increasingly difficult to travel the long distance between her home and the Bahá'í Centre. On 23 May 1931, the anniversary of the declaration of the Báb, she passed away.

Without delay the 'devoted, able promoter and pioneer of the Faith'[136] Annie Romer cabled the distressing news to the Guardian and then to Alfred Lunt, secretary of the National Spiritual Assembly of the United States and Canada.

Claudia's funeral took place on 27 May at her home at Warwick Gardens which 'appeared to have been turned, on the day of the funeral, into a garden of flowers'.[137] A number of notable Bahá'ís, among them Lady Blomfield, Mary Hanford Ford and Beatrice Irwin, took part in the service. Two messages were read, one from the Guardian and the other from the American Bahá'ís. Shoghi Effendi cabled:

> Deeply grieved passing such staunch, indefatigable worker. Assure her daughter, relatives, friends heartfelt condolences, fervent prayers.[138]

At the end of the service the friends travelled to the little country cemetery on Bledlow Ridge near her daughter's cottage. In the warm and sunny afternoon prayers were said at the graveside and Claudia's body interred.

In the following weeks all of the large Bahá'í communities in North America held memorial services for Claudia. On 28 August 1931 St Barbe wrote to Claudia's daughter:

> I cannot tell you how distressed I am to hear of your sad loss. Your dear Mother was one in a million and just the most choice soul it has ever been my privilege to know. She will be missed by countless friends, seen and unseen. Her influence reached very far and thousands she had never seen knew of her devotion and held her in deep regard. I shall always remember her wonderful spirit. There was that sense of supreme understanding. A light shone from her eyes and from her being there radiated an atmosphere which pertained to the divine.
>
> I shall miss her more than I can now tell and all other 'Men of the Trees' will realize their great loss – words fail to describe my feelings. To me her life was nearer perfection than any other I have known.[139]

For Claudia's granddaughter, these words are an expression of her grandmother's true essence.[140]

3

Anna Kunz

Anna Kunz was the eldest of three children. At the time of her birth on 13 July 1889 in the parsonage of Aber Entfelden, Aargua, Switzerland, her father, the Reverend Adolph Bolliger, was already a prominent clergyman in the Reformed Church. Soon afterwards he was appointed professor of theology at the University of Basel and some years later he became its president.[141]

Anna's childhood was hard. At one time her mother had two servants to look after the family but because she thought that they spent too much time amusing each other, she decided to keep only one. When Anna had grown up sufficiently to do housework, her mother dismissed the remaining servant. For about a year afterwards Anna did all the housework except ironing and clothes washing. Her daughter Annamarie commented, 'It was hard work, and had she continued, she might have cracked under the strain.'[142]

Anna also did the shopping, walking 30 minutes to the market and taking longer on the way home, owing to the heavy loads she had to carry.[143] She also had to entertain her little brothers and sisters, sometimes taking them to the zoo in the afternoon so that they could play together away from home.[144]

When life at home was particularly difficult Anna's mother used to sing. Annamarie has suggested that 'Perhaps she was calling on her soul to cling to God.'[145]

For a month each summer Anna's father left Basel to act as travelling minister in one holiday resort or other. Although he had certain duties to perform, he enjoyed what was essentially a holiday. Anna was Reverend Bollinger's favourite child and he liked to have her accompany him to the train station and carry his suitcase. Anna would weep as she said goodbye to him and this show of emotion gave him pleasure. His family, however, was relieved when he was away.

Although the Reverend Bolliger usually took his vacation alone, one summer he took his wife with him because she was unwell. On their return to Basel they found that he had been invited to become the minister at the Newmunster Church in Zurich.

Anna's father was uncertain whether or not to accept the invitation, so every day for several weeks the whole family prayed on their knees that he would make the right decision. In the end he decided to take the new position and in the autumn of 1905 the family moved to Zurich.

When Anna graduated from high school she wanted to attend university. However, her father did not approve of the idea, even objecting to her leaving home. When a friend of the family offered to pay Anna's expenses, the Reverend Bolliger changed his mind and consented to her taking a course in domestic training at a seminary in Bern.

Anna studied at the seminary for a year and a half. At the end of this time she remained at the seminary for another year to teach handicraft. Although she had a full schedule, the work required of her was not as hard as the work she had done at home.[146]

Anna's husband, Jakob Kunz, was born on 3 November 1874 in Brittnau, Aargau, Switzerland. His father worked his own farm and occasionally did weaving at a factory or at home on a hand loom.[147] Jakob was so poor he once had to wear his aunt's shoes to school.[148]

Jakob received his education in the public schools, supporting himself at the gymnasium by tutoring. In 1897 he received a Bachelor of Science at the polytechnic in Zurich and for the next three years he worked as a chemist in Basel. He then returned to the polytechnic in Zurich as an instructor in physics. He received a Ph.D. in 1902 but continued to work at the polytechnic until 1907.[149]

Whenever Jakob was in Zurich he visited the Bolliger home, greatly enjoying his talks with Anna's theologian father and the company of her family.[150] Jakob spent the winter of 1907-8 in Cambridge, England, where he undertook research work at the Cavendish Laboratory. At Cambridge he met Dean Thomas F. Halgate of Northwestern University, who promised to help him find a position in America if Jakob ever came to that country. Early the following summer, after he had made a brief visit to Zurich, Jakob decided to take advantage of his new friend's offer.[151]

By this time Anna was 19 and had become a beautiful and attractive young woman. Jakob left for America with the promise that he would write to her often.

Late in the summer of 1908, with little money, Jakob arrived in Evanston, Illinois, and reminded Dean Halgate of his promise. After some difficulty, he secured Jakob a position as an instructor in physics at the University of Michigan.

Before he had completed one year of teaching there Jakob was offered an assistant professorship. At the same time, President Edmund J. James of the University of Illinois, who was looking for a certain degree of European influence in the rapidly developing graduate programme of that institution, made Jakob a more attractive offer of an assistant professorship in mathematical physics. Jakob took up this offer, soon becoming an associate professor and eventually a full one.[152]

Jakob and Anna became engaged through their correspondence. In the spring of 1913 Jakob made a trip to Switzerland, going immediately to Zurich to see Anna. Although at first they planned to be married in August, they asked Anna's father to marry them in July, which he agreed to do. Soon after their wedding Jakob returned to Urbana, Illinois, with Anna.

When President and Mrs James met Anna they were immediately impressed with her unusual charm and physical beauty.[153] According to her daughter Margaret, Anna loved her new country from the beginning and often told stories about the wonderfully kind way in which the people of Urbana treated her when she arrived as a bride. Used to a conservative, traditional way of life in Switzerland, she was overwhelmed by the hospitality and generosity of the Americans. Anna gradually learned the new style of living, as well as a new language.[154]

Almost 52 years later, in May 1965, when she was once again living in Zurich, Anna wrote to her grandson Chris Ruhe-Schoen:

> I feel compelled to call back the early days when I came to America. Your grandfather took me to the Methodist Church where I met many kind people, and one evening I remember clearly, he said he was going to another church, but he did not think that I would be interested. However, I wanted to go with him and thus we went together to the Unitarian Church at the corner of Matthews and Oregon Street where the Reverend Vail conducted an evening class for students and townspeople. After a short talk there was always a lively discussion and your grandfather loved them. Mr Vail had had a great experience the year before (in 1912) when he met 'Abdu'l-Bahá, and as a Unitarian minister it was hard for him to hold back the wonders of that meeting. Many times he would refer to it and we finally went during the winter of 1913-1914 to his sermons on Sunday morning when he was carried by a spirit hard to describe . . . even I was uplifted to unknown heights even though I was struggling with a foreign language.
>
> Slowly Mr Vail selected some of his class to meet especially to hear about 'Abdu'l-Bahá and the Bahá'í Faith and we saw more and more of Mr & Mrs Vail . . . it must have been 1916 when I could say to the Vails that I believed, before this I always had times when I said frankly that Christ was sufficient . . .[155]

During the spring of 1920, at the start of Jakob's first sabbatical leave, he and Anna travelled to Zurich with their two baby daughters, Annamarie and Margaret. Of that time Anna has written:

> For fifteen months we were guests of your great-grandfather who was at that time still a minister at the Newmunster and we lived in the parsonage next to the church. It was not always easy to stand up for a new Faith, but I must say that your grandfather and I stood together and we soon telegraphed 'Abdu'l-Bahá for permission to go to Haifa. He in turn granted our wish, but suggested postponing our pilgrimage until the spring of 1921, saying that the heat in the summer would be hard on us. We, as all early believers, were anxious to do something for the Faith so that while in Switzerland we got in touch with Mason Remey who was then in good standing and travelling in Europe. He came and lectured in the big hall of the Karl der Grosse. We made all the arrangements and found a fine translator in Frau Consul Schwarz of Stuttgart. The hall was well filled and we invited people to come for the day after to tea in the same building in a small, lovely room. Quite a number came, Mason and we talked to them and from that group we arranged for a weekly get-together in the same restaurant. Jakob helped faithfully with the meetings when he was in Zurich but he soon went to Munich where he studied with Professor Sommerfeld.
>
> For me it was no little undertaking to conduct these classes, but my love for the Faith, and for 'Abdu'l-Bahá, gave me the strength. I had to leave your great-grandfather's house quietly without making mention of where I was going. However, in that class were some of the ones who became the upholders of the first Zurich Bahá'í Community. One or two had heard of the Faith through Professor Forel in Lausanne, and Madame Vautier, for many years the backbone of Zurich, appeared after having heard in a train about these classes.[156]

Dr Auguste Forel, the famous Swiss entomologist and psychiatrist, first heard of the Bahá'í Faith in 1920 at Karlsruhe.

He became a Bahá'í late in 1921 after reading a Tablet revealed for him by 'Abdu'l-Bahá.[157]

Anna and Jakob went on pilgrimage in the spring of 1921, as suggested by 'Abdu'l-Bahá. Anna's account of the journey appeared in *Star of the West*:

> It was just a few minutes before midnight of March twenty-second, 1921, when the 'Karlsbad' entered the blessed harbour of Haifa, dropping anchor about a mile off the shore. The full moon stood bright and glorious over Mount Carmel . . . Early in the morning my husband and I were met by Dr Lotfullah Hakim, whom Abdul Baha had sent. Abdul Baha was not at Haifa. After a severe illness he had gone to Tiberias for a rest. In his absence, we were beautifully taken care of by his family and friends. Awaiting Abdul Baha's further instructions as to when we should be permitted to meet him, we enjoyed Haifa and Acca.
>
> . . . Shortly after our arrival we were climbing over the rocky path to the Tomb of the Bab . . . As one enters that sanctuary one feels at once in union with the higher world. As we knelt there in prayer my heart seemed to melt; there was but one great longing. When we prayed there for the last time . . . it was as if my heart would break.[158]

On the morning of Good Friday Anna and Jakob went with members of the Master's family and a few other Bahá'ís to the Bahá'í holy places in 'Akká and Bahjí. From the station in 'Akká they walked through the green meadows past the Mansion of Bahjí to the little house in which the pilgrims always rested before entering the Tomb. They then entered the Shrine of Bahá'u'lláh:

> The place was filled with the fragrance of Jasmine blossoms, a heavenly light filled the room. Here we felt at once at rest and were permitted to pray for our friends, for the world, whose saviour had come as a thief in the night. Here heaven and earth seemed to meet . . . Tears were welcome, they brought relief to the heart so overfull. Everybody slowly withdrew, leaving Mr Kunz and myself alone at the Holy Shrine, whence for ages to come people of all classes, races and religions will derive new strength and assurance of God's nearness.[159]

On Saturday morning Jakob and Anna travelled from Haifa to Tiberias where the Master awaited them. On the day of their arrival they only caught a 'few glimpses' of Him but on Easter morning He called them into His room:

> Though I feared to approach him, after his loving words of welcome this fear vanished . . . His look seems to go into one's very heart . . . To us his outward appearance seemed similar to that of the old Hebrew Prophets; his humility, his simplicity and love were like the Christ . . . Abdul Baha talked to us with a ringing, piercing voice which will forever sound in my ears. His words would come forth with that unique simplicity, then he would pause for a while, often closing his eyes. His spirit, it seemed when I dared to look at him, had left his body; he was looking into infinitude, communing with that world for which we long . . .[160]

When early on Monday morning Anna and Jakob showed 'Abdu'l-Bahá a photograph of their children 'his beautiful face lighted up'. 'They have bright faces,' He said, after looking at the photograph for a long while. 'They will be real Bahais because they will have a Bahai education. They will become good Bahais.'[161]

While in Tiberias Jakob and Anna asked the Master many questions, particularly about science. For example, they asked, 'Science denies immortality. How does the prophet know the contrary?' 'Abdu'l-Bahá replied in part:

> Science does not know; but the Manifestation makes discoveries with the power of the Spirit . . . the Manifestations see with their inner eye (own eye); they do not go from premises to conclusions. The prophets see many things with their inner eye. They do not need to go by discoveries. The scientist with induction is like a blind man who cannot see two steps ahead of him. The prophet sees a long distance.[162]

They also asked 'Abdu'l-Bahá what the requisites were for a successful meeting. 'Before the meeting you must pray and supplicate for divine assistance,' He replied.[163] 'Why is there so much evil in the world?' they wanted to know. 'Abdu'l-Bahá answered:

God has created a remedy for every disease. One must apply the remedy. Now these patients run away from the expert physician. They neglect him. Under inexperienced physicians they get worse. The words of the religious leaders have no influence, no effect. These physicians are more diseased than their patients. The spiritual leaders now have no faith, though they claim to have faith in order to secure their positions.[164]

On 28 March 'Abdu'l-Bahá revealed a prayer for the Kunz children:

He is God!

O God! Make Thou these sweet children, Anne Maria Kunz and Margaret Rosa Kunz, brilliant and heavenly and rear them up in the bosom of (Thy) grace so that they may, like unto two pearls in the mother-pearl of Bahá'í education, attain to the utmost lustre and luminosity and that the light of (Thine) infinite favour may shine forth from their foreheads. Verily, thou art the Giver, the Bestower and the Affectionate.[165]

On Tuesday morning, 29 March, Anna and Jakob had their last meeting with 'Abdu'l-Bahá. He told them:

You have been here three days. They are equal to three years . . . The results of this visit will be equal to the results of three years. Now you should go back in perfect harmony and joy and with supreme glad tidings. You should gladden the hearts with glad tidings of the Beauty of Abha. Say to the friends: 'The Kingdom of God has been opened to you. The tree of life is yours. Heavenly graces are bestowed upon you. The effulgence of the Sun of Truth is shed on you. God has chosen you. This crown He has placed upon your head. This eternal life has been given you. Therefore you should be very happy. Turn day and night to the Kingdom of Abha. Supplicate for boundless favours from that Kingdom.' . . . We are all His servants, drawing light from the Sun of Abha.[166]

Anna and Jakob reluctantly returned to Zurich, their hearts 'near to breaking'.[167] On 30 May the Master revealed this Tablet for them:

To the dear daughter Mrs Kunz, and Mr Kunz, unto them
be the Glory of God, the Most Glorious. He is the most
Glorious. O ye two heavenly birds!
From Switzerland ye took flight unto the Holy Land and
again did ye return thereto. Praise be unto God that we met
one another, that the utmost affection manifested, and the
oneness of hearts and souls shone forth!
Your visit with 'Abdu'l-Bahá was like unto the contact of
the candle with the fire which became immediately lighted.
This is a proof of great capacity. It is my hope that those
two candles will become day by day brighter and brighter
and these two birds will soar higher and higher till they will
attain to the infinite plane of the Kingdom. Unto you be
Abhá Glory![168]

Shortly after Jakob and Anna returned to Zurich Jakob
left for Munich to continue his studies with Professor
Sommerfeld. While in Munich he visited a number of Bahá'í
communities, telling them the story of his pilgrimage. Anna
continued to hold her Bahá'í classes in Zurich.[169] When they
returned to Urbana in the early autumn they served the
Cause with renewed enthusiasm, spurred no doubt by this
Tablet revealed for them by the Master on 8 October:

He is God!
O ye two firm ones in the Covenant!
Your letter has been received from Zurich. The contents
were very eloquent. Praise be to God that in Germany ye
established meetings which were in the utmost spirituality,
were confirmed in the service of the Kingdom of God,
attracted some souls and gave assurance to the hearts. It is
my hope that in America ye may also raise the banner,
breathe into the people the breaths of life, release them
from the darkness of error, illumine them with the light of
guidance; good news may come from you, which may be the
cause of joy to the heart and fragrant breaths may be dif-
fused from you which may scent the nostrils.
Upon ye be the Glory of Abhá![170]

Both Jakob and Anna served on the Spiritual Assembly of Urbana. After the Master suddenly passed away on 28 November 1921, Jakob became confused. Although he loved 'Abdu'l-Bahá deeply, he came under the false impression that the Bahá'í Cause was not to be organized; as a result he slowly grew away from the Faith.[171] His personal attributes were, however, undiminished:

> Kunz had the proverbial simplicity of a true scientist; he was liberal in politics and religion, and was always an enthusiastic worker for social justice. It used to be a puzzle why, either at home or on an expedition, the cranks and queer people were attracted to him as to a magnet. On analysis this was seen to be due to his kindly nature, for he would listen patiently to everybody, no matter how absurd their views, and such interviews were naturally repeated.
>
> He was never really Americanized in many ways, such for instance as in driving an automobile. He considered a bicycle plenty good enough for the half mile between home and office, and who shall say he was not right? He did not enjoy ordinary sports or games, in fact he never learned to play much of anything, but he did like to work in his garden. He was not interested in trivial things, but was always ready for a good strenuous discussion on philosophy, religion or politics.[172]

Jakob's daughter Margaret has described some of his scientific achievements, saying that he 'became famous as the inventor of the first photo-electric cell, later known as the "Kunz cell"'; in collaboration with Professor Tykociner he helped to develop the first sound motion pictures. 'He measured the light of the solar corona at the time of the solar eclipses' and 'taught relativity as propounded by his colleague Albert Einstein'.[173]

The disappointing realization that her gifted husband for some reason did not understand the Bahá'í Administrative Order in no way diminished Anna's deep love for the Cause of God or her passionate desire to serve it. A member of the Spiritual Assembly for a number of years and often its chairman, Anna was regularly elected a delegate to the national convention of the Bahá'ís of the United States and Canada. Through her attendance at such events Anna became well acquainted with more than a few Bahá'ís. According to Margaret, 'the friends respected' her mother's 'knowledge of the Teachings, her wisdom and common sense'.[174]

Margaret has related that her mother was shining and radiant, 'with piercing brown eyes', and that she had a great joy of life. Although conscientious in her Bahá'í work, she still maintained a balanced attitude towards it. Leaving her duties for a day or two, 'she would often jump into her car and drive out into the countryside' where she would take long walks. She would then return to her work with renewed joy and enthusiasm.[175]

Anna loved flowers and always kept her garden in beautiful shape. When her daughters were little she frequently asked them to take bouquets to their neighbours and friends.[176]

A strict disciplinarian and a believer in the law of reward and punishment, Anna expected her daughters to live by all of the teachings of the Bahá'í Faith. Fully aware that the high standard of morality expected of a Bahá'í was in strong contrast to what went on in the world generally, she advised them 'to have the courage to be different'. Although she never hesitated to punish her children when she felt that they deserved it, Anna was a warm and loving mother and was very affectionate towards them.[177]

Like Anna, who was her close friend, the distinguished Bahá'í teacher Mabel Hyde Paine, compiler of *The Divine Art of Living*, first heard of the Bahá'í Cause from Albert Vail. She too became a believer in 1916. Mabel's daughter Sylvia Parmelee loved Anna very much and remembers her well:

> Rather regal in manner, she held her head erect in a way that commanded respect and attention. People almost instinctively turned to her for advice and guidance in personal matters . . . As chairman of the Local Assembly of

Urbana she guided the consultations but never dominated them. She gave all of its members a chance to express their opinions, but when it became evident that they were getting too tired, she brought them promptly to a close. She used to say that the Assembly could not make wise decisions after ten o'clock in the evening.

. . . Anna was an impeccable hostess. She served everyone personally and there was always an abundance of simple delicious refreshments. Her home was gracious and inviting. She held many firesides there. The friends sat in the front living room. Although Jakob seldom attended them, from his study in the adjoining room he listened intently to what was being said. Many of the Bahá'ís from Urbana, both youth and adult, received their inspiration and desire to become believers in the Kunz's home.[178]

Many Bahá'í teachers, as well as philosophers and scientists, spent their nights at the Kunz home. Louis Gregory, a well-known Bahá'í and future Hand of the Cause, was a frequent visitor. Jakob took particular pleasure in the company of this noble and much-loved man.[179] Margaret recalls looking out of her window one day when she was a young girl and seeing her mother 'on the way to a Bahá'í function, walking side by side with Louis Gregory'. She wondered what people would think when they saw her distinguished and very white mother ambling along with the distinguished and very brown Mr Gregory – but such a thought never seemed to occur to her mother at all.[180]

Jakob earned a sabbatical every seven years and he and his family 'went back to the old home, he to renew his studies, usually with Sommerfeld at Munich to get the latest application of quantum theory and wave mechanics'.[181] In the summer of 1928 Jakob began his second sabbatical leave. While he renewed his studies with Professor Sommerfeld, Anna and the children went to stay with her parents in Zurich.

Although Anna's mother felt very close to Jesus and could not imagine life without Him, her husband did not understand the station of a Manifestation of God and believed in approaching God directly. When he became depressed, however, or was faced with serious problems, he realized that something in his religion was missing and he would then turn to the Salvation Army for comfort. While Anna was staying with him on this occasion he read part of John Esslemont's *Bahá'u'lláh and the New Era*. He was apparently unimpressed with the book for he said to Anna before she left that she had better give up the Bahá'í Faith. 'Have you ever known a Bolliger to give up what he or she believed in?' was her reply.[182]

Meanwhile, Jakob became more and more opposed to the Bahá'í Administrative Order. Although he considered some of the Bahá'ís to be his close friends, he did not approve of his wife's deep involvement with the Faith. In the 1930s he strongly objected when his daughters wished to attend the recently-established Bahá'í summer school at Louhelen Ranch near Davison, Michigan, but owing to Anna's insistence they went there just the same.[183] At the same time, Anna did all she could to make her husband's life smooth and happy, sometimes even accompanying him to church.[184]

According to his grandson, Jakob only read serious literature; Dante, Schiller and Goethe were among his favourite authors. Although her husband was scornful of the *Reader's Digest*, Anna enjoyed the brief articles and read the magazine quite regularly. Annamarie and Margaret were, however, forbidden by their father to read comic books.[185]

During the last few years of his life Jakob was warned several times to work at a slower pace. This he did but only with reluctance. He was engaged in important projects until a few weeks before his death from a heart attack on 18 July 1938 at the age of 64. His biographer Joel Stebbins called him 'a sincere scientist, a true internationalist, and a faithful friend'.[186] Anna later wrote of him, 'At times I felt that he was, in practical life, more a Bahá'í than his wife, or some of our best travelling speakers . . . I believe in God's mercy, and let us believe that in another world he has now found the truth.'[187]

Anna was 49 when Jakob died. Although she undoubtedly missed him, for they loved one another very much, she now felt free to give all her time and energy to serving the Bahá'í Cause. She learned to type so that she could do secretarial work for the Bahá'ís and, having learned to drive some years before, was able to take Bahá'ís and inquirers to meetings. Anna's earliest attempts at driving were not wholly successful. Margaret recounted this story to her son Chris:

> Your grandmother had just learned to drive, and one wintry morning as she drove along with me the car skidded violently on some ice. As the car spun around your grandmother pronounced, 'Now it has happened: the steering wheel has broken!'[188]

In 1939 Annamarie married John O. Honnold, who became a distinguished professor of law. Margaret followed suit by marrying Dr David Ruhe in 1940. Dr Ruhe had a successful medical career until his election as secretary of the National Spiritual Assembly of the United States in 1963. Five years later he was elected to the Universal House of Justice on which he served until 1993. Anna was extremely pleased that her daughters had married such fine and gifted men and became increasingly proud of her sons-in-law.

Anna's daughters had now left home and although she never lacked for visitors, Anna was the only permanent resident in her formal and attractive house. When Shoghi Effendi announced in his letter of 5 June 1946 that Switzerland was to be added to the list of those European countries which were to raise up new spiritual assemblies in the second Seven Year Plan,[189] Anna responded. Less than a year later she asked the Guardian if she might pioneer to her native land. After receiving his enthusiastic approval, on 26 July 1947, at the age of 58, Anna sailed to Oslo. From there she travelled to Basel and then to Bern.

A compilation of her letters to her daughters entitled 'A Bahá'í in Switzerland' provides an insight into her experiences there:

I go nowhere without stating the purpose of my stay in
Bern. When I am told that the third world war is inevitable,
and it happens often, I take the opportunity to say the
Bahá'ís are working to prevent this. 'Utopia,' they say, until
one is able to show how we hope to influence human hearts.
But it is true that the materialism here in Switzerland is as
dangerously developed as in the United States . . . We
continue to work and we shall repel every thought of war
with a thought of peace. The work at its best will be slow,
but with Bahá'u'lláh guiding and leading His army we
cannot doubt victory. Eventual success will be achieved in
His name! (19 September)[190]

Through publicity and through the Esperanto group, Fritzi
Shaver and Elsa Steinmetz, the first two pioneers from
America to Bern, have made friends who are willing to study
the Faith. One advertisement brought ten inquiries for
literature and further information. Together we are leading
the study class once a week. (30 September)[191]

Fritzi and Elsa were known as the 'inseparable sisters'. They
had arrived in Bern on 7 April 1947 and together with four
Bahá'ís who had travelled from Geneva to meet them held
the first Nineteen Day Feast in Bern that same day.[192]

On 14 October 1947 Rúḥíyyih Khánum wrote to Anna
on behalf of Shoghi Effendi:

Dear Bahá'í Sister,
Our beloved Guardian was delighted to learn in your
letter of September 19th that you are now active at your
pioneer post in Switzerland. He feels sure that your services
will be of the greatest help there.
You asked for his suggestions. He is particularly anxious
that the group in Zurich should get all the help that it can
and that an assembly should be established there in addition to one in Bern. He, therefore, urges you to visit it and
help the friends there as often as possible. Likewise, any
visits that you can make to Geneva will, no doubt, stimulate
the contacts made there, and help Mrs Lynch and Mrs
Graeffe in the excellent work they are doing.
You may be sure that he will pray for your dear daughters and for their husbands as well . . .

What you are doing for the Cause is very deeply valued by him, and he will certainly pray for the speedy realization of all your hopes for your native land.
With warmest Bahá'í love,
R. Rabbani

The Guardian added to this letter a most encouraging message:

Dear and valued co-worker,
I welcome your arrival in Europe and particularly in Switzerland where, I feel, your work will be of the utmost value. You will surely be blessed and sustained in your historic task, and I look forward to the day when through your exertions and those of your devoted collaborators the first assembly will be established in that land. Persevere in your magnificent mission.
Your true and grateful brother,
Shoghi[193]

Later that month Anna wrote to her daughter:

We always serve after each meeting in order to have a good social hour with our students. I think the young people on Friday enjoyed it greatly. Fritzi and Elsa are very nice hostesses and I feel that the Swiss people love it and are amazed by it. Balancing a cup on the lap is, however, still not very much appreciated here. They still prefer gathering around the table.[194]

Anna's letter to Annamarie and Margaret on 28 January the next year was almost entirely composed of this reflection:

We all have limitations as to strength and time and unless we find time to dwell daily on the creative word, read and meditate, we cut ourselves off from that life giving spirit which alone can attract others to that Faith which we represent and love. In this material age of ours it is hard enough to find the balance and I know how hard it is to battle and how difficult it is to feel God's nearness.[195]

On 13 March Anna wrote:

Just now my school friend left my room . . . She actually
came to ask whether I thought her worthy of becoming a
Bahá'í . . . but I made her feel how great a blessing it must
be to become the first Bahá'í in a city . . . Fritzi just now
phoned the happy news that another inquirer . . . has spent
the afternoon with her and Elsa and wanted to sign as a
Bahá'í . . . Your prayers are needed . . . in order that perhaps an assembly may arise on April 21st.[196]

A month later, on 23 April, Anna informed her daughters:

We pioneers are naturally happy that on the twenty-first we
were able to organize our Assembly. We made quite a little
occasion of it . . . In Geneva, too, they have organized.[197]

The first European Teaching conference took place in
Geneva from 22 to 26 May 1948, attended by 92 Bahá'ís
from 19 countries. Shoghi Effendi sent a message that
'created the spiritual reality' of the historic occasion. He said,
in part:

Overjoyed at the manifold signs of the rapid progress
evidenced by the formation of eight Assemblies in seven
goal countries, in the notable increase in the number of new
believers, in the remarkable activity displayed by itinerant
teachers and the meritorious endeavour systematically
exerted by the organizers and participators of the newly
launched European campaign in the opening years of the
Second Seven Year Plan.[198]

In her letter of 29 May to Annamarie and Margaret, Anna
remarked:

Our Geneva Conference belongs to the past and, when we
have recovered from our physical fatigue, the blessing of
the days spent together will so fill our souls with thanksgiv-
ing that it will stand in our memories as a shining occasion
in our Bahá'í lives.[199]

A year later, on 21 July 1949, Rúḥíyyih Khánum wrote on
behalf of the Guardian:

Your letter of June 23rd was received and our beloved Guardian has instructed me to answer you in his behalf.

The wonderful and self-sacrificing work you have done in Switzerland he very deeply appreciates and admires, and there is no doubt that the Bern Assembly is now firmly enough established for you to leave it and return to America. Wherever the Bahá'ís are the tasks to be done seem, and indeed, are unending, so there will be no lack of work for you to do when you get home.

He urges you to tell the American friends about the work and the new Bahá'ís in Europe. These new believers, with the well-balanced minds of the Europeans, are a fine type, and in return for what they have been given by their American brethren, have much to contribute of maturity and wisdom.

Shoghi Effendi added his message:

Dear and valued co-worker,

The services you have rendered the Faith are truly remarkable and deserve the highest praise. I feel truly proud of your achievements and am grateful for the spirit that so powerfully animates you in the service of our glorious Faith. I will pray ardently on your behalf that the Beloved may abundantly reward you for your accomplishment and enable you in the years to come to enrich the splendid record of your services to His Faith and its institutions.

Your true and grateful brother,
Shoghi[200]

Soon after receiving this letter Anna returned to her home in Urbana.

The Guardian did not originally include as an object of the Second Seven Year Plan the formation of a National Spiritual Assembly for Italy and Switzerland. However, in his message to the Bahá'ís of 8 March 1952 he announced that he had instructed Ugo Giachery, in conjunction with the European Teaching Committee, to take immediate steps to establish this assembly. He continued:

Appeal to the American Bahá'í community, particularly the Bahá'ís residing in Italy and Switzerland, to exert their utmost to insure in the course of the coming year the multiplication of Spiritual Assemblies in both countries, thereby broadening the basis of the projected pillar of the future Universal House of Justice.[201]

Anna undoubtedly read this moving appeal with great interest. When news reached her that pioneers were urgently needed in Switzerland she felt, as her daughter Margaret has described, 'restless and torn'. Anna's personal longing and wish was to be near her beloved daughters and their children. Not knowing what she should do, she wrote to the Guardian for advice. Much to her relief, he did not answer her for a long time.

Then came his stunning reply: 'Proceed as quickly as possible to Switzerland.' Although crushed by his answer, in October 1952 she again left Urbana for her native country, settling in Zurich.[202]

The first Italo-Swiss convention took place in Florence from 23 to 26 April 1953 to form the 'Twelfth Pillar of the Universal House of Justice'. The Guardian's message to the convention expressed his 'joy, pride' and 'gratitude' at the progress of the Cause in the two countries and gave the new assembly two functions: to stimulate the propagation of the Faith and to consolidate it. He attached ten specific tasks for the assembly to undertake, from the incorporation of the national assembly and the local spiritual assemblies to the establishment of summer schools.[203]

On Saturday 25 April the new national assembly was elected. Anna was elected secretary and her home in Zurich became the national Bahá'í office.[204]

Margaret Kunz-Ruhe relates that her mother was at first somewhat distressed to learn that she had been elected to such an important and demanding office as secretary of a new national assembly,[205] particularly given her age, just three months short of 64. However, as Daniel Schaubacher said later:

Never before had she considered herself worthy of or capable of assuming and fulfilling an administrative position. Despite this, she followed the call with obedience, resolution and bravery . . . It meant the start of a new life . . . The instructive and loving mother . . . became an expert administrator who carried out her duties with skill and dignity.[206]

Anna's home in Zurich remained the national Bahá'í headquarters for two years. Then, in obedience to the Guardian's request, she left her attractive apartment, of which she had grown very fond, and moved to Bern so that she could be near the new Bahá'í centre.[207]

Not only was Bern to be the site of the Bahá'í offices, it was also to be the location of the future Mashriqu'l-Adhkár of Switzerland. Shoghi Effendi loved Switzerland and spent many of his holidays there. Rúḥíyyih Khánum relates this story:

The last year of the Guardian's life two Swiss pilgrims came to Haifa. Their presence stirred up all his memories of Switzerland and his love for their country poured out in a manner wholly unlike his usual reserve about his personal life and feelings . . . He was moved to inform them that he wished Switzerland to have its own Temple site, which was to be situated near the capital city of Bern and have a clear view of the Bernese Alps, where he had spent so many months of his life walking and climbing.[208]

On 12 August 1957 his secretary wrote to the National Spiritual Assembly of Italy and Switzerland:

As he explained to . . . he is very anxious for Switzerland to purchase a plot, however small in size, and modest a beginning it may be, for the future Mashriqu'l-Adhkár of that country . . . he is very happy to be able to present this land himself to the Swiss Community.[209]

Rúḥíyyih Khánum notes that 'this was a gift of a unique nature, no other community in the Bahá'í world having been thus honoured'.[210]

Anna had often wished to meet the beloved Guardian but for some reason, known perhaps only to herself, she never had this priceless experience. She did, however, attend his funeral in London in November 1957, overcoming her fear of flying in order to be present.

In April 1962, 'after nine years of fruitful cooperation with the Italian friends, the Swiss believers held their own first convention in Bern in the presence of Hand of the Cause Ugo Giachery'.[211] Anna was elected secretary of the new National Spiritual Assembly of Switzerland. She continued to serve on that body until 1969, when she retired owing to her age – nearly 80 – and her weak physical condition.[212]

Throughout her time in Switzerland Anna enjoyed a close relationship with her brothers and sisters, whom she loved. Although they did not understand the Bahá'í Faith nor why Anna had given her life to it, they still looked up to her and often turned to her for comfort and advice.[213]

Shortly before Riḍván 1963, Anna, accompanied by her son-in-law Dr David Ruhe, a member of the American National Spiritual Assembly, travelled to the Holy Land as a delegate to the first international Bahá'í convention. It was her first visit since she had met the Master there in 1921. On the morning of 21 April, which marked the hundredth anniversary of the declaration of Bahá'u'lláh, Anna and David joined nearly three hundred members of 56 National Spiritual Assemblies in the House of the Master to share the precious experience of electing the first Universal House of Justice.

Anna's last years were plagued by a series of illnesses. As Daniel Schaubacher related:

> Because of her age and physical frailty, Anna soon had to limit her involvement. On no account did this mean inactivity, however . . . She remained in close contact with her circle of friends and the Bahá'í world. She supported the sick, her grandchildren, her daughters, all of her loved ones and the advancement of God's word through her daily prayers. To visit her was a blessing . . .[214]

One day in the summer of 1973 Anna received a letter from Margaret saying that she and David had just arrived in Iran where they hoped to visit the Bahá'í holy places and see the Bahá'ís. When Anna read the letter she said to her nurse, 'I am overjoyed,' but then said she felt very tired. Her frail body could no longer support so much excitement and joy; she had suffered a stroke. On the morning of 10 August she died peacefully in her sleep.

Annamarie immediately flew from America to Bern and, with much difficulty, contacted Margaret, who arrived just in time for her mother's funeral.[215] The Universal House of Justice cabled this message to the National Spiritual Assembly of Switzerland:

> Deeply grieved passing distinguished handmaid Bahá'u'lláh her association beloved Master devoted pioneering service Europe over extended period unforgettable . . .[216]

Memorial services for Anna were held at the House of Worship in Wilmette, at the home of Hand of the Cause Roy Wilhelm in West Englewood, New Jersey, and in Urbana, Rome and Langenhain, Germany.[217] A few days after the funeral Dr Giachery wrote to the Universal House of Justice:

> Once more in the course of this year we must offer you our deepest condolence for the loss of a much loved and distinguished collaborator, Mrs Anna Kunz, whose services in this continent shall be remembered for many decades to come . . .[I] had the opportunity and privilege to work side by side with her and to appreciate her sterling qualities, her deep love for the Cause and her high sense of responsibility in discharging the duties of the 12th National Assembly of the Bahá'í World. Her kind and loving attitude towards everybody, her wise and her humane approach to so many novel problems, made of Mrs Kunz one of the best national secretaries in Europe. We mourn her loss, but pray that her noble soul may reap the reward due to those who laboured so faithfully for the Cause of God.[218]

Annemarie remarks in the preface to her book *Vignettes from the Life of 'Abdu'l-Bahá* that she is 'deeply grateful' to her mother, who led her to 'spiritual birth'.[219] No doubt many others whose lives were touched by Anna Kunz would express the same sentiments.

4

Amelia Collins

Shortly before noon on 9 July 1951 Sara Kenny hurried into the large meeting room of the Bahá'í Centre on New Hampshire Avenue in downtown Los Angeles. With obvious pleasure and quiet excitement she told the Bahá'ís gathered, 'Mrs Collins is here!' The friends received this news with surprise and delight. Although I had been a member of the Bahá'í community for only a little over a year and knew almost nothing about Mrs Collins and her services to the Faith, I was nevertheless anxious to meet the person whose unexpected presence was the cause of such interest and pleasure.

Mrs Collins entered just as the commemoration of the anniversary of the martyrdom of the Báb was about to begin. She had a strong face with a warm, kind expression and was simply dressed in black. When the devotional programme was completed she moved to a chair in the corner of the room, somewhat apart from the other Bahá'ís.

Amelia Engelder Collins was born on 7 June 1873 in Pittsburgh, Pennsylvania. The seventh child in a family of 14, she had nine brothers and four sisters. Her father, Conrad Engelder, who as a young man had left Germany to live in the United States, had married the American born Catherine Groff and become a Lutheran clergyman. A very strict parent, he often punished Amelia and his other children, sometimes insisting that they learn by heart a chapter of the Bible. Amelia, however, was possessed of a naturally strong character and was not afraid to stand up to him. Some of her brothers followed in their father's footsteps and became clergymen.

Those close to and fond of Amelia always called her Milly. When Milly was a young girl, she and her brothers visited a friend in Copper Harbor, Michigan. Here she met Thomas H. Collins, whom she later married.

Milly and Tom spent the first few years of their married life in Calumet, Michigan. Tom then suggested that they move to Bisbee, Arizona, where he had mining interests. He warned Milly that they would have to live in somewhat primitive conditions but instead of objecting to this prospect as other women might have done, Milly looked forward to it as a stimulating challenge. Tom made a fortune from mining, which the couple used to help educate their nieces and nephews, having no children of their own.

It seems that while Tom was serving his country in Paris in World War I he fell in love with a nurse. On his return to the United States he asked Milly for a divorce. Deeply shocked by his request, she flatly refused to grant it. He was furious and vowed that he would leave her virtually nothing in his will.[220] Milly did not change her mind. Her spiritual strength and adherence to high principles saved their marriage.

In 1917 Nellie Stevison French, the wife of Tom's business partner, became a confirmed Bahá'í through Isabella Brittingham, who was travelling in Arizona. Mrs French had first heard of the Bahá'í Faith in 1896 when she and her mother had attended a few Bahá'í meetings in Chicago and she had kept up a sporadic interest. Now she became the 'first resident Bahá'í teacher in Arizona'.[221]

The next year the Frenches moved to Pasadena, California, and the Collinses soon followed. Shortly after Milly and Tom moved into their new home, Nellie spoke to Milly about the Bahá'í Cause. Milly became a Bahá'í in 1919.

Milly's first Bahá'í friends advised her to write a letter to 'Abdu'l-Bahá and 'beg for confirmation and strength'. After spending a restless night of uncertainty wondering how to do this, she finally 'scribbled something'. Then in the morning, opening her curtains and seeing the light pouring in, she thought to herself, 'The sun shines on the world and all that is therein with such grandeur and liberality; does it need a letter?' and tore up her note, 'certain that the spirit of the beloved Master, 'Abdu'l-Bahá, also would shine upon the world of human beings and grant them faith and love'.[222]

Some days later, much to her astonishment, she received a Tablet from 'Abdu'l-Bahá, addressed to 'O thou lady of the Kingdom'. It read, in part:

> In brief, from the bounties of His Holiness Bahá'u'lláh, My hope is that thou mayest daily advance in the Kingdom, that thou mayest become a heavenly soul, confirmed by the breaths of the Holy Spirit, and may erect a structure that shall eternally remain firm and unshakable.[223]

Milly did not show this Tablet to anyone for some time.[224]

'Abdu'l-Bahá passed away in the early hours of the morning of 28 November 1921. In His Will He had appointed Shoghi Effendi Guardian of the Bahá'í Faith. Amelia used to say, 'After the provisions of His Will became known, my whole heart and soul turned to that youthful Branch, appointed by Him to watch over and guide the Faith of Bahá'u'lláh. How I prayed that God would help me to make him happy!'[225]

Early in 1923 Amelia made her first pilgrimage to the Holy Land. Tom went with her, although he was not a Bahá'í. They planned to stay in a hotel but the Guardian invited them to stay in the pilgrim house.

Towards the end of the Master's life a Persian believer had given 'Abdu'l-Bahá a piece of land opposite His home in Haifa. While on pilgrimage in 1919 the American Bahá'í William H. Randall had asked 'Abdu'l-Bahá if he might finance the building of a pilgrim house for the Western believers on this land. Both these offers were accepted. Draft plans were drawn up which were corrected and altered by 'Abdu'l-Bahá until a final design was evolved and approved by Him. Construction of the building was begun before the passing of 'Abdu'l-Bahá, but the Randall family fell into financial difficulties and the funds provided were insufficient to carry on the work. When the Collinses arrived in 1923 the building was still unfinished. Milly related later:

> My husband was not a Bahá'í, but after two or three days of my pilgrimage he became so enthralled with love for the Guardian that one day, while looking at the new and uncompleted building of the Western Pilgrim House, he became angry and exclaimed, 'How can the Bahá'ís see an unfinished building every day in front of the Guardian's eyes? You will see that the building is brought to completion.'[226]

Thus Milly, together with seven other Bahá'ís, contributed towards the completion of the building, which served as a Western Pilgrim House until 1963, when it became the temporary seat of the Universal House of Justice and later of the International Teaching Centre.

Milly's father had died when she was a little girl. Before the lid of his coffin was closed she had been taken to have a last look at him. One night during her pilgrimage she dreamt that she was standing beside her father's coffin and that he 'arose . . . as if awakened'. This frightened Milly so much that she woke up 'very perplexed'. The next morning, in a state of great agitation at the prospect of meeting Bahá'u'lláh's daughter for the first time, Milly entered the presence of the Greatest Holy Leaf. During their conversation, the Greatest Holy Leaf asked Milly, 'Did you have a dream?' On being asked a second time Milly suddenly remembered her dream and told Bahíyyih <u>Kh</u>ánum about it. 'Of course,' the Greatest Holy Leaf said with a smile, 'your faith in this Cause has brought your father back to life again.'[227]

Before Milly had met the Guardian her 'sole aim' had been 'to learn from him some truths about prayer, and purification of the soul and heart'. She used to tell the friends, 'To me he was a door to the world beyond, and through him I longed to have a glimpse of that wondrous world.'[228]

One evening during her pilgrimage the Guardian gave Milly some papers to study. With great eagerness she went to her room to read them. She was greatly disappointed to discover, however, that they contained only 'explanations and elucidations of the World Order of Bahá'u'lláh and how it should be established'. When Shoghi Effendi asked her the next day what she thought of the documents, she was unable to speak anything except the truth: 'What shall I say? I did not understand anything!'[229]

The Guardian asked her to walk with him through the lanes near his house and patiently explained to her the subjects about which he had written. Privately Milly hoped that he would speak to her of the mysteries of prayer but rather he 'began to educate' her in the principles of Bahá'í administration.[230]

When Milly returned home she went immediately to the fifteenth annual national Bahá'í convention. She arrived just as the chairman was reading out the very letter that she had been asked to study in Haifa. Its concluding paragraphs carried a weighty message:

> The need for the centralization of authority in the National Spiritual Assembly, and the concentration of power in the various local Assemblies, is made manifest when we reflect that the Cause of Bahá'u'lláh is still in its age of tender growth and in a stage of transition; when we remember that the full implications and the exact significance of the Master's world-wide instructions, as laid down in His Will, are as yet not fully grasped, and the whole Movement has not sufficiently crystallized in the eyes of the world.
>
> It is our primary task to keep the most vigilant eye on the manner and character of its growth, to combat effectively the forces of separation and of sectarian tendencies, lest the Spirit of the Cause be obscured, its unity be threatened, its Teachings suffer corruption; lest extreme orthodoxy on one hand, and irresponsible freedom on the other, cause it to deviate from that Straight Path which alone can lead it to success.

But let us be on our guard – so the Master continually reminds us from His Station on high – lest too much concern in that which is secondary in importance, and too long a preoccupation with the details of our affairs and activities, make us neglectful of the most essential, the most urgent of all our obligations, namely, to bury our cares and teach the Cause, delivering far and wide this Message of Salvation to a sorely-stricken world.[231]

According to Louis Gregory, who recorded the events of the convention, 'the high call to service, the divine order, harmony, and enthusiasm of this letter riveted the attention of the delegates and laid the foundation for the deliberations during the next three days'.[232]

The Guardian had brought about a great change in Milly. Now able to grasp the meaning of his letter, she was anxious to share with others his thoughts about it. 'I found myself called to the front, and the words that I spoke came from some deep well of consciousness.'[233]

In the communities she visited after the convention Milly found the Bahá'ís had made the letter the basis of their serious discussion. When they disagreed about its contents, Milly found she had been 'prepared by the beloved Guardian to explain and throw light upon' the subject and tried to dispel their misconceptions.[234]

In 1924 Milly and Tom took a cruise to Scandinavia, stopping in Reykjavik for two days. As the ship on which they travelled was the largest one ever to have entered that harbour, the Icelanders celebrated its landing with a holiday. While Milly was visiting the Einar Jónsson Museum she met Hómfrídur Arnadóttir, a 51-year old women well known for her humanitarian services. Through Milly's guidance and warm friendship she became the first Icelandic Bahá'í.[235]

Later that year the National Spiritual Assembly appointed a Finance Committee to help the Bahá'ís understand the needs of the national fund. Each of its five members represented a different region of the North American continent and was to answer questions about the fund from the friends in his region. Milly represented the Western states, serving on this committee with distinction.[236] In later years Milly served on a number of other committees, including the National Teaching, Assembly Development and the Inter-American Committees.

In 1925 the seventeenth annual convention and Bahá'í congress took place at Green Acre in Eliot, Maine from 4 to 9 July. At the convention Milly was elected to the National Spiritual Assembly of the United States and Canada, along with Horace Holley, Florence Morton, Siegfried Schopflocher, Mountfort Mills, Roy Wilhelm, Allen McDaniel, Carl Scheffler and Ali Kuli Khan. Thus she found herself, 'very young in the Cause, sitting with old, accomplished and learned friends'. Although she had 'initial fears', she soon overcame them and added greatly to the consultations of that body for a number of years.[237]

When she was on pilgrimage the Guardian advised Milly always to show kindness and love to her husband. She tried to follow this advice, saying that she never disobeyed Tom.[238] The friends often begged Milly to stay another night after a meeting so that she could give a Bahá'í talk or attend some gathering, but she always refused the invitation, preferring to return home to Tom immediately.[239]

Milly sometimes accompanied Tom on his business trips. While he was engaged with his work, she would often visit the Bahá'ís. Rosemary Sala has related this story: When the Collinses were travelling during the nineteen days of the fast, Milly, shortly before dawn, would take some fruit and biscuits into the bathroom or a large clothes closet, eat her breakfast and then say her prayers. One morning Tom discovered what she was doing and scolded her severely for disregarding her health. He then ordered room service to bring his wife breakfast every morning at the hour she wished.[240]

Tom liked to hunt and fish and he also enjoyed good food. In 1927, however, he suffered a serious heart attack and was unable to carry out these activities. When he fell ill Milly cared for and nursed him. One day when he was lying on a couch he asked her to open a drawer in his desk and bring him a certain envelope. The envelope, he told her with tears in his eyes, contained his will – he had left everything he owned entirely to her.[241]

Beginning early in her Bahá'í life the Guardian often sent Milly letters of encouragement and high praise for what he called her 'magnificent endeavours for the propagation of the Bahá'í Faith'.[242] In 1926 Milly was able to send a large sum of money to the Holy Land which was much needed for the development of the Bahá'í institutions there. The Guardian wrote to her in response:

> I am inexpressibly touched by this further evidence of your spontaneous and self-sacrificing devotion. I will devote your generous donation to promote such interests of the Cause as are most vital and nearest and dearest to my heart . . . Your bright and shining example is I am certain acclaimed and glorified by the Supreme Concourse in the Abhá Kingdom and in this world below you have undoubtedly earned the affection and the admiration of us all. With deepest and truest love to my unforgettable friend and brother Mr Collins. Your grateful brother, Shoghi.[243]

Milly and Tom helped develop a Bahá'í summer school at the home of John and Louise Bosch in Geyserville, California. Early in 1927 the National Spiritual Assembly appointed a committee of John, Leroy Ioas and George Latimer to make plans for the establishment of just such a school in the Western states. Many years before, the Boschs had written to 'Abdu'l-Bahá saying that they wished to 'dedicate their lovely fruit ranch as a centre for universal service where mankind might partake of the spiritual teachings of Bahá'u'lláh'. Now they offered their home and ranch as the summer school. About 130 Bahá'ís 'gathered under the majestic pine tree' on the Feast of Asmá' in August 1927 to launch the first summer school.[244]

Every year the attendance at the school increased and the courses of study became more comprehensive. For the first eight years John and Louise were host and hostess to the Bahá'ís and charged them nothing for their board and lodgings. In 1935 the Boschs deeded their property to the National Spiritual Assembly. The next year, knowing that the summer school needed more facilities, Milly and Tom erected and presented an attractive hall of rustic redwood suitable for the holding of study classes and public meetings. Collins Hall, as it became known, was dedicated in a simple and impressive ceremony on 12 July 1936. A cablegram from Shoghi Effendi was read:

> Heartily join celebration opening Auditorium generously founded by well beloved distinguished friends Mr and Mrs Collins. Assure them profound abiding gratitude. Love assembled friends.[245]

At the time the Collinses were in Bad Nauheim and were unable to attend the ceremony. Milly sent a cable, however, the reading of which closed the meeting: 'Utmost gratitude for the Name that has taught us there is no separation.'[246]

The next year Milly and Tom made another much-needed gift to Geyserville summer school: a fully equipped dormitory for fifty persons built, like the hall, from rustic redwood.

Later that year, while on another trip to Europe, Tom suddenly died on board ship. Milly brought his remains back to the United States. 'At this bitter moment of my life', she later said, 'I received such a bounty from the Guardian that all my sorrow came to an end':

> Greatly distressed sudden passing beloved husband. Heart overflowing tenderest sympathy. Offering special prayers. Advising Geyserville summer school hold befitting memorial gathering recognition generous support their institution. May Beloved aid him attain goal he was steadily approaching closing years of his life.[247]

On 3 July 1937 the new dormitory at Geyserville was dedicated following the annual reunion and Feast. After the dedication, which was attended by about 250 people, Leroy Ioas conducted a moving memorial service for Mr Collins.[248]

In November 1937 Milly made a second pilgrimage to the Holy Land. She was a friend of May Bolles Maxwell, whose daughter Mary had married the Guardian in March 1937. On this pilgrimage Millie began a close and significant friendship with Rúḥíyyih Khánum, as Shoghi Effendi's wife was afterwards known. It was while she was on this pilgrimage that the Guardian told Milly, 'Your husband is in the presence of the Master and is proud of your services.'[249]

When she left the Holy Land Milly carried with her a sacred gift from the Guardian for the American Bahá'í community. In his cable of 27 April 1938 addressed to the thirtieth American convention, the Guardian wrote:

> As token my gratitude to such community entrusted beloved co-worker Mrs Collins locks Bahá'u'lláh's most precious hair arranged preserved by loving hands Greatest Holy Leaf to rest beneath dome of Temple nobly raised by dearly loved believers in American continent.[250]

As Beatrice Ashton has related, Milly presented the Guardian's gift, which she had 'beautifully framed and placed in a special silver case', to the officers of the convention.[251]

At this convention Milly was elected to the American National Assembly for the first time since 1933. She remained on it without interruption until early in 1951 when the Guardian invited her to serve at the World Centre.

On 3 July 1938, under the same pine tree that had witnessed all the opening sessions at Geyserville, the twelfth annual school began with a feast of unity. About two hundred Bahá'ís were present. In her short address Milly said to the friends, 'The peace and calm prevailing at Geyserville instils higher joy and happiness.' She conveyed to them the Guardian's hope 'that this school would typify the ideal Bahá'í community in all phases of its sessions and life'.[252]

Rosemary Sala told this charming story about Milly. Some months after Tom's passing, Milly decided to sell her attractive house in California and move to Wilmette, Illinois. One morning Charles Laughton telephoned Milly for permission to see her house. At nine o'clock that night, he and his wife, Elsa Lancaster, both dressed in evening clothes, arrived at Milly's front door. Since Milly seldom saw a film or went to the theatre, she did not know that she was meeting two famous people. Much impressed with her house, Mr Laughton remarked on the fine atmosphere that she had created in it and expressed the hope that he and his wife would succeed in doing the same. After the Laughtons had left, Milly's housekeeper explained to her who they were. A few evenings later, Mr Laughton called again and offered Milly an absurdly low price for her house. Since she was in a hurry to sell it, she accepted the offer without hesitation. Mr Laughton then asked her what, if anything, she would like him to recite for her. In reply she suggested the Gettysburg address and the 23rd Psalm. After he had willingly agreed to do this, Milly took him into her garden. There in the moonlight and with the sea behind him he recited these pieces for Milly – for her, an unforgettable experience.

A few years later, when Milly was visiting California, she called at her old home. Although Mr Laughton was in bed with the flu, he told his housekeeper that he wished to see Mrs Collins. At his request she sat beside him and he held her hand. He told her that 'his conscience had been troubling him for the shabby way in which he had forced her to take so little for her house and asked her if he could make restitution'. Milly suggested that he might like to give the difference to the European Children's Fund, which he promised to do.[253]

On 24 January 1940, towards the end of the third year of the first Seven Year Plan launched by Shoghi Effendi to spread the Faith throughout North and South America, May Bolles Maxwell, at the age of 70, left her comfortable home in Montreal and, accompanied by her 'precious niece' Jeanne Bolles, sailed on the SS *Brazil* for Buenos Aires. Her purpose was to assist the believers there to establish firmly the newly-formed Bahá'í community. On the afternoon of 1 March, only three days after she had arrived in the city, May died of an illness of just a few hours' duration.[254] On hearing the tragic news, Shoghi Effendi cabled Sutherland Maxwell:

> Grieve profoundly yet comforted abiding realization befitting end so noble career valiant exemplary service Cause Bahá'u'lláh. Rúḥíyyih though acutely conscious irreparable loss rejoices reverently grateful immortal crown deservedly won her illustrious mother. Advise internment Buenos Aires. Her tomb designed by yourself erected by me spot she fell gloriously will become historic centre pioneer Bahá'í activity. Most welcome arrange affairs reside Haifa. Be assured deepest loving sympathy.[255]

By the beginning of June 1942 the National Spiritual Assembly of the United States and Canada had received from Mr Maxwell, who was now living in the Holy Land, his design for the proposed monument and, from the Bahá'í Committee of Buenos Aires, a sample of fine Carrara marble. Deciding not to rely on correspondence that was bound to be difficult and might well prove unsatisfactory, the National Assembly asked Milly to consult and work with the Bahá'í Committee of Buenos Aires so that the plans for May's monument might be 'faithfully and properly fulfilled'. As soon as the Assembly received the consent of Shoghi Effendi, Milly, who had never been to that continent before, prepared to leave for South America. Compelled to postpone her trip three times because a government at war needed her seat on the plane, and obliged to travel by boat and train most of the way, Milly arrived at Buenos Aires a few weeks after sailing from New Orleans on 24 September.

In her own account of her experience, Milly wrote with engaging simplicity:

> While standing at the hotel desk filling out the questionnaire required of visitors a momentary feeling of loneliness passed over me as I realized that I was in a country where

I did not speak the same language of those about me. Suddenly the porter said, 'You are Mrs Collins' and handed me a cablegram. The message was from Shoghi Effendi and read, 'Prayers accompany you always, everywhere. Deepest loving appreciation.' Immediately I felt at home in spite of the fact that on account of many delays the friends in Buenos Aires did not know of my arrival.[256]

The next day, Sunday, Milly and some of the friends had lunch with Señor Formos and his wife in the garden of their country home. As they sat together under the trees and spoke about the Bahá'í teachings, their spirit of unity increased until they were as one in their 'purpose to share with others the spiritual bounties showered upon the world by Bahá'u'lláh'.[257]

On the following day Señor Formos and Señor Barros inspected the huge block of Carrara marble from which the sample seen by the American National Assembly had been taken. After a careful search for a suitable sculptor, they awarded a contract to Mario Viciana, an Italian, to make a model in plaster of the proposed monument. Much pleased with his work, they engaged him to construct the monument itself. Milly frequently visited the sculptor's studio to see how the work was progressing and often went to May's grave to plan the erection of the monument.[258]

Milly recalled that the friends in Buenos Aires showed her much kindness and consideration, remarking that owing to their efforts articles explaining her mission appeared in both the Spanish and English newspapers and on the radio.

After six weeks Milly was convinced that the work on the monument could be completed without her further assistance. On 'a bright morning in December', she boarded a plane for Rio de Janeiro. Here she stayed for two days, spending 'happy hours at the home of a pioneer' and meeting 'many delightful young people'.[259] On her return to Wilmette, the Guardian wrote to her:

Dear and prized co-worker:
Your voyage to South America at this critical hour, the efforts you have exerted for the initiation of the construction of May's memorial are indeed outstanding and never-to-be-forgotten achievements that enrich still further the magnificent record of your services, local, national, as well as international, so nobly rendered to the Cause of Bahá'u'lláh and its rising institutions. The Bahá'ís, East and West, North and South, admire and are thankful for such signal services . . . Be happy and persevere in your exemplary and historic services. Affectionately, Shoghi.[260]

On 30 May 1943, about five months after Milly's visit, with the impressive monument already in place, the Bahá'ís of Buenos Aires held a moving ceremony at May's grave.

At the end of the second world war, Hómfrídur Arnadóttir, whom Milly had led to the Faith in 1924, invited Milly to live in Iceland. Hómfrídur had translated John Esslemont's classic text book of the Bahá'í Faith, *Bahá'u'lláh and the New Era*, into Icelandic and Milly had provided the money for its publication. Now Milly wrote to the Guardian asking what she should do. He replied, through his secretary:

As he cabled you, he feels your presence in America more important than Iceland at this time . . . The small assemblies in America are badly in need of Bahá'í education. People like you, who are loving, tactful and wise, to help them see their problems and the solution for them, should be in continual circulation, so to speak. Again he would remind you not to overtax your strength or wear yourself out in your desire to do all you can for the work. Your services are too much needed for you to jeopardize your health . . .[261]

Milly's frequent and extensive travels for the Cause took her to Bahá'í centres in the United States and Canada, where she helped to consolidate the believers; to Central and South America, where she encouraged the teaching work; and, after the second world war, to Britain, Poland, Switzerland and Germany, where she stimulated the friends and promoted the Faith.[262]

Emogene Hoagg

Claudia Stuart Coles

Anna Kunz, *centre*, with her daughter Margaret and son-in-law David Ruhe

Amelia Collins

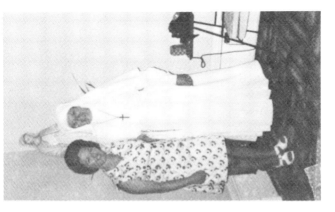

Left Kate Dwyer, *centre*, with Helen Pirkins, *right*, and Mahvash Master, *left*
Right Kate Dwyer, *right*, before she became a Bahá'í

Ella M. Bailey

Ella Quant, 1923

Party for Marion Holley, 1945, before she left for England to marry David Hofman
Standing left to right: 2. Ramona Brown. 3. Kathryn Frankland. 8. Anna Kunz. 12. Mildred Nichols. 13. Marion Holley. 14. Mari Yazdi, 15. Charlotte Linfoot. *Sitting left to right:* 1. Ella Bailey, 2. Mrs Carpenter, 3. Barbara Yazdi

According to Rosemary Sala, Milly visited her nephew while he was serving as the American Consul in Poland. Much to her disappointment, she could not openly teach the Faith or even say the world 'Bahá'í' to a Pole, but as she walked along the streets and sat in the parks, she silently called upon Bahá'u'lláh to help all those who came near her.[263]

The Guardian sometimes gave Milly special missions. She would instantly obey his instructions and then give him a confidential report.

In His Will and Testament 'Abdu'l-Bahá had written: 'O friends! The Hands of the Cause of God must be nominated and appointed by the Guardian of the Cause of God. All must be under his shadow and obey his command.'[264] From the beginning of his ministry until 24 December 1951 when he announced the first contingent of Hands, Shoghi Effendi conferred this exalted station on certain believers only after their passing, with one exception. On 22 November 1946 he sent this cable to Milly:

> Your magnificent international services, exemplary devotion, and now this signal service impel me inform you your elevation rank Hand Cause Bahá'u'lláh. You are first be told this honour in lifetime. As to time announcement leave it my discretion.[265]

The following January he wrote in the postscript to a letter written on his behalf:

> You have acquitted yourself of the task I felt prompted to impose upon you in a manner that deserves the praise of the Concourse on high. The high rank you now occupy and which no Bahá'í has ever held in his own lifetime has been conferred solely in recognition of the manifold services you have already rendered, and is, by no means, intended to be a stimulus or encouragement in the path of service. Indeed the character of this latest and highly significant service you have rendered places you in the category of the Chosen

Nine who, unlike the other Hands of the Cause, are to be associated directly and intimately with the cares and responsibilities of the Guardian of the Faith. I feel truly proud of you, am drawn closer to you, and admire more deeply than ever before the spirit that animates you.[266]

The exact nature of Milly's 'highly significant service' is not described in the letters of the Guardian, but towards the end of 1947 he wrote to her:

The memory of the services, assistance and support you extended to me in my hour of anxiety and stress a year ago at this time, is still vivid, and evokes my deepest admiration and gratitude.[267]

On 8 April 1916, while in the garden outside the Shrine of Bahá'u'lláh, 'Abdu'l-Bahá revealed one of the Tablets of the Divine Plan. In those dark hours of the first world war, He assigned to the believers an important mission:

Attach great importance to the indigenous population of America. For these souls may be likened unto the ancient inhabitants of the Arabian Peninsula, who, prior to the Mission of Muḥammad, were like unto savages. When the light of Muḥammad shone forth in their midst, however, they became so radiant as to illumine the world. Likewise, these Indians, should they be educated and guided, there can be no doubt that they will become so illumined as to enlighten the whole earth.[268]

Milly was one of the first to respond to this call. For many years she not only deputized certain believers to teach the Omaha Indians in Macy, Nebraska, but often visited them herself. In 1948 the first Indian local assembly in America was formed in Macy.[269]

In January 1949 Milly and delegates from seven South American countries attended the third South American Teaching Congress in Sao Paulo, Brazil. In his report to the *Bahá'í News*, Esteban Canales wrote:

The congress has been a complete success and this because of the wonderful spirit which pervaded it, the enormous work accomplished by the delegates, the assistance given by the marvellous Sao Paulo Community, and especially the fine help which we received through the presence of Mrs Amelia Collins.[270]

According to her brief account of her journey given to the Committee for Latin American News, the Bahá'ís of Sao Paulo took full advantage of the opportunity offered it by the Congress by holding local meetings and gaining publicity. A stimulating public meeting held in the municipal library attracted a large number of people. Owing to the wonderful cooperation of the press, several fine articles about the Congress appeared in the newspapers. Milly remarked on the dedication of the delegates and the eagerness of all the Latin American friends to assume increasing responsibility for the progress of the Cause.[271]

Before returning to her home in March, Milly visited seven communities in South America and two in Central America.

In November 1950 Milly received a cable from the Guardian. Rúḥíyyih Khánum relates:

Quite suddenly, one day in Switzerland in November 1950 . . . the Guardian sat down and, to my great astonishment, sent cables inviting the first of that group who later became members of the International Bahá'í Council to come to Haifa.[272]

Milly, the Revell sisters – Ethel and Jessie – Lotfullah Hakim and Mason Remey joined Shoghi Effendi in the Holy Land about a month later. One evening at dinner in the Western Pilgrim House the Guardian told them and Ben and Gladys Weeden, who had been serving at the World Centre for some months, that he planned to constitute, from the group, the International Bahá'í Council. In January 1951 he announced his decision to the Bahá'í world:

Proclaim National Assemblies of East and West weighty epoch-making decision of formation of first International Bahá'í Council, forerunner of supreme administrative institution destined to emerge in fullness of time within precincts beneath shadow of World Spiritual Centre of Faith already established in twin cities of 'Akká and Haifa . . . Nascent Institution now created is invested with threefold function: first, to forge link with authorities of newly emerged State; second, to assist me to discharge responsibilities involved in erection of mighty superstructure of the Báb's Holy Shrine; third, to conduct negotiations related to matters of personal status with civil authorities.[273]

On 2 March of that same year the Guardian wrote to the friends of East and West:

Greatly welcome assistance of the newly-formed International Council, particularly its President, Mason Remey, and its Vice-President, Amelia Collins, through contact with authorities designed to spread the fame, consolidate the foundations and widen the scope of influence emanating from the twin spiritual, administrative World Centres permanently fixed in the Holy Land constituting the midmost heart of the entire planet.[274]

Now that Milly was serving on the Council, the Guardian invited her to live permanently in Haifa. For over a year, except when travelling at Shoghi Effendi's request or attending to her personal affairs, she lived in the company of the other members of that institution at the Western Pilgrim House.

In his message of 24 December 1951 to the Bahá'í world, after describing a 'chain of recent historic events' in the Holy Land and outlining his plans for the future of the Cause, the Guardian announced:

Hour now ripe to take long inevitably deferred step in conformity with provisions of 'Abdu'l-Bahá's Testament . . . through appointment of first contingent of Hands of Cause of God, twelve in number, equally allocated Holy Land, Asiatic, American, European continents.[275]

Milly's name was among those appointed in the Holy Land. Milly's room in the Western Pilgrim House was rather damp, which exacerbated her arthritis. After the death of Hand of the Cause Sutherland Maxwell on 22 March 1952, Shoghi Effendi invited Milly to move into the Master's house and occupy the vacant room.[276] Rúḥíyyih Khánum provides a moving description of Milly's relationship with the Guardian:

> So great and tender was her love for Shoghi Effendi . . . that she almost never wrote to him directly but addressed her letters to me in order to spare him the necessity of writing to her direct . . . her every thought was directed to sparing him, in any way she could, the slightest extra effort and to serving him in any way that could bring some happiness to his heart. So great was her concern in these matters that, although she lived in his house, when the time came for him to go out or come in she would return to her room so as not to oblige him to expend a moment of his over-taxed time and tired mind on greeting her and feeling he should stop to talk to her for a few minutes. Sometimes her age and ailments would confine her to her room and then the Guardian would pay her a visit for a few moments, often bringing her a gift . . . he came one evening when she was ill and took from his own neck the soft warm cashmere shawl a Bahá'í had given him and placed it himself about hers. It became her most treasured possession and she could never forget the touch of the warmth of his neck on hers.[277]

Ethel Revell wrote that Milly's 'happiness always was in being near the Guardian and that sometimes when she was talking in her room and she could hear him moving in his room which was directly above hers, she would interrupt her conversation and say "that was the Guardian's footstep"'.[278]

As the Guardian grew older and his heavy burden increased still further, Rúḥíyyih Khánum tried to persuade him to be a little easier on himself and, when he travelled, to do so in at least modest comfort. Milly shared this concern and 'formed the habit of offering him a sum of money' before he left for his annual trip away from the Holy Land. Only after 'vehement appeals' from his wife would he consent to put aside a small amount of the money for himself – he always spent the rest on 'purchases for the gardens, Holy Places and Archives'.[279]

Ever since childhood Milly had loved gates and wanted to have one of her own. After becoming a Bahá'í, however, she lost interest in material possessions and forgot her desire to own a gate. One day after she had been called to work in the Holy Land she received a note from Shoghi Effendi together with a photograph of an impressive wrought iron gate. In his note he asked her how she liked the gate. It had been bought with money she had offered him for his personal needs. Milly immediately replied to the Guardian. 'Exceedingly beautiful.'

One evening in the spring of 1952, while at dinner at the Western Pilgrim House, William Foster, a builder and contractor, asked the Guardian if he could be of some service while on pilgrimage. Shoghi Effendi asked him if he could erect the 'Collins Gate' in the Ḥaram-i-Aqdas, the area around the Shrine of Bahá'u'lláh. Hearing the name 'Collins Gate' for the first time, Milly 'gazed at the beloved Guardian, the Sign of God on earth, who knew her inmost longing'. 'He knew that my life had no worth', she later said, 'except to offer at his bidding at any moment. He responded to my look with a heavenly smile.'[280]

Before returning to his pioneering post in Africa, Mr Foster erected the magnificent gate at the entrance to the broad path leading to the Shrine of Bahá'u'lláh. Bahá'í pilgrims and visitors now pass through the Collins Gate as they draw near to the holiest spot on earth.

In his message of 30 November 1951 to all National Spiritual Assemblies, the Guardian announced that in 1953, to celebrate the hundredth anniversary of the revelation of Bahá'u'lláh in the dungeon of the Síyáh-Chál in Tehran, four intercontinental Bahá'í teaching conferences would be 'held successively' in Africa, America, Europe and Asia.[281] The next year, on 8 October, he revealed his plan to launch a 'world-embracing Spiritual Crusade' at these conferences. He explained that the four objectives of the Crusade were the development of 'the institutions at the World Centre of the Faith in the Holy Land', consolidation 'of the twelve territories destined to serve as administrative bases for the operations of the twelve National Plans', the 'consolidation of all territories already opened to the Faith' and 'the opening of the remaining chief virgin territories on the planet'.[282]

Milly had already learned of this great venture one night in the pilgrim house. The Guardian had been unwell for a few days and had been unable to meet with the friends. On his first evening back, while at dinner, he told Milly and the others of the great 'Spiritual Crusade'. While listening to him Milly thought of the words of the Greatest Holy Leaf, who had often remarked that the Guardian's hands resembled those of Bahá'u'lláh. Later that evening, Shoghi Effendi unrolled a map showing the goals of the Crusade; Milly's eyes were fixed on the 'rhythmic movement of his beautiful hands and fingers'.[283] Wishing to serve, Milly immediately asked, 'Where can I go?' but the Guardian replied, 'Your place is here.'[284]

The All-American International Teaching Conference, called by the Guardian the 'most distinguished of the four',[285] took place in the Medinah Temple in Chicago from 3 to 6 May 1953. On 1 May some 2,500 people attended the Consecration Service of the Mother Temple of the West in Wilmette, marking the occasion on which 'Abdu'l-Bahá, 51 years before, had laid its foundation stone.[286]

Milly accompanied Rúḥíyyih Khánum, who was delegated by the Guardian to deliver his official message and 'elucidate the character and purposes of the impending decade-long spiritual World Crusade and rally the participants to energetic, sustained, enthusiastic prosecution of the colossal tasks ahead'. They were also 'to bear, for the edification of the attendants, a precious remembrance of the Co-founder of the Faith'.[287] In addition, Shoghi Effendi asked Rúḥíyyih

<u>Kh</u>ánum and Milly to 'carry, on my behalf, to unveil on the occasion of the completion of the construction of the Mother Temple of the West, to the privileged attendants at the Wilmette Conference a most prized remembrance of the Author of the Faith, which never before left the shores of the Holy Land, to be placed beneath the dome of the consecrated edifice'.[288] This gift was a 'coloured, photographically reproduced Portrait of Bahá'u'lláh "in the bloom of manhood"' painted by a Christian artist who had seen Bahá'u'lláh at the public bath at Baghdad.[289]

Rúḥíyyih <u>Kh</u>ánum was further assigned the task of acting as Shoghi Effendi's deputy 'at the historic ceremony marking the official Dedication of the holiest Ma<u>sh</u>riqu'l-A<u>dh</u>kár of the Bahá'í world'.[290]

In the afternoon of the third day of the conference, Milly opened the consultation on the role of youth in the Crusade. Reading the words of the Guardian, she said that they offered the 'key for all of us today':

> The magnetic power is the action of the believers. If they arise and show the right spirit it will act as a magnet and attract this power which is accumulated ready to aid every believer who will arise to serve.[291]

On the afternoon of the fourth and last day of the conference Rúḥíyyih <u>Kh</u>ánum 'aroused the spirit of pioneering with her stirring talk entitled 'Mount Your Steeds!'[292] Following this talk, Milly concluded the conference with some brief remarks:

> Now I have witnessed in this audience day after day your great joy, your inspiration, your longing to serve, the pledges you have made, and all of this I feel is the result of our Guardian's sacrifice. Let us just cherish this thought all through the next ten years, that our Guardian is sacrificing for us daily, and with great joy. To see the Guardian smile just once is enough to cause you to wish to lay down your life . . .[293]

Milly then closed the conference by reading the Tablet of Visitation revealed by 'Abdu'l-Bahá.

After the conference Milly and Rúḥíyyih Khánum travelled to Montreal to attend a memorial service which the Guardian had instructed the Montreal Bahá'ís to hold at Sutherland Maxwell's grave. Before returning to the Holy Land, Rúḥíyyih Khánum turned her parents' house over to the National Spiritual Assembly of Canada, as had been their wish. This house, designed by Rúḥíyyih Khánum's father, had been visited by the Master several times, the only house in Canada to be so blessed.[294]

From 21 to 26 July 1953 Milly attended the third Intercontinental Bahá'í Teaching Conference in Stockholm. Held in the large and attractive auditorium of the Citizen's Hall, the conference hosted 14 Hands of the Cause and 374 others from 30 countries.

At the start of the afternoon session on Saturday 25 July, Milly, obeying the request of the Guardian, showed recent photographs of the nearly-completed Shrine of the Báb on Mount Carmel. She told the friends that on the first day of Riḍván Shoghi Effendi had sealed behind one of the golden tiles on the dome of the shrine a bit of plaster from the ceiling of the room in which the Báb had been a prisoner in Máh-Kú.[295]

In the early years of his ministry Shoghi Effendi had conceived the plan of erecting a House of Worship on the highest point of the western end of Mount Carmel, as near as possible to the spot where on one of His four visits to that holy mountain Bahá'u'lláh had pitched His tent and revealed the majestic and prophetic Tablet of Carmel. Early in the 1950s Shoghi Effendi requested Leroy Ioas, Hand of the Cause and Secretary-General of the International Bahá'í Council, to make the necessary arrangements for the purchase of the land and some of the land surrounding it. As soon as Milly learned of this, she 'begged' Shoghi Effendi 'to allow her to donate the money for its purchase'. She later said 'that if she ever received any reward in this transient life, this was it'.[296]

It was on the afternoon of the first day of the fourth Intercontinental Teaching Conference, held from 7 to 15 October 1953 in New Delhi, that the Guardian cabled:

> ... preliminary steps have been taken, aiming at the acquisition of an extensive area at the head of the holy mountain, scene of the revelation of the Tablet of Carmel, preparatory to the purchase of the site for the future Mother Mashriqu'l-Adhkár of the Holy Land, made possible by the munificent hundred thousand dollar donation of the Hand of the Cause, Amelia Collins, signalizing the opening of the second stage in the unfoldment of the mighty process set in motion by the Author of the Faith.[297]

In his classic study of the Guardian, Hand of the Cause Ugo Giachery recalled:

> I was at that Conference and remember the joy and enthusiasm of the friends who voted to send Mrs Collins the following telegram: 'Conference joyfully voted one voice express admiration abiding gratitude your generous gift land Mashriqu'l-Adhkár holy mountain.'[298]

Early in December 1954 while on her way back from the United States to the Holy Land, Milly stayed for a few days in New York City. On the evening of 11 December the Feast of Questions was held in the rather dreary Hotel Parkside overlooking the attractive and historic Gramercy Park. There I met Milly for the second time.

After being introduced, she said directly to me, 'I hear that you are going on pilgrimage next month.'

'Oh, yes,' I said, with natural enthusiasm.

'That it very nice,' she said. 'You will be most welcome. I look forward to seeing you in Haifa.'

Her kind, sincere tone and look of real interest affected me most pleasantly.

On my first day at lunch in the Western Pilgrim House, Milly occupied a seat next to Rúhíyyih Khánum, almost directly opposite the main entrance to the dining room. Conversation was warm and spontaneous. Those present seemed happy and at ease. Rúḥíyyih Khánum mentioned that a large contribution was needed for a certain project. She said to Mrs Collins affectionately, 'Now, Milly, it is your turn to speak.'

'There is a limit to what I can do,' Milly said a little seriously.

Rúḥíyyih Khánum assured her, 'I was only joking!'

The Guardian knew that Milly had been suffering from arthritis in her hands for some time. One evening just after the friends had joined him for dinner, he leaned a little towards her across the table and asked with much concern, 'Are your hands better?' I could not hear her somewhat hesitant answer. Then he vigorously assured her, 'They are better.'

Late on the last afternoon of my pilgrimage Milly invited me to her room in the Master's house. Although the room was attractive it lacked modern conveniences. After we were comfortably seated, she said simply, 'I can afford every luxury and yet I am deeply grateful to be living here.'

She spoke about Tom, her husband, with both affection and amusement and mentioned that he had never discouraged her from doing Bahá'í work. She also said to me:

Tom always permitted Bahá'ís to visit us provided they behaved as he thought that they should. Once Mrs Brittingham came to stay with my husband and myself in California before he had met many Bahá'ís. The morning after her arrival I made a particular effort to prepare what I thought would be a delicious breakfast. When she came into the dining room and looked at the table, she said with some distress, 'Oh! but the Master told me to eat apples!' My husband politely suggested to her that perhaps she would be more comfortable in a hotel.

On another occasion when Martha Root spent the night at our house, she kept my husband waiting for well over an hour for breakfast. When she did arrive downstairs, instead of apologizing, she put her arm around his neck and said, 'Tom, I have been praying for you for an hour and a half.' He did not accept her excuse.

After we talked together for about 15 minutes Milly led me into the room where the Master had ascended. Peaceful and happy, I did not realize that I was raising my voice. Milly advised me gently, 'Speak more quietly. The Guardian might come through the hallway and hear you.'

At her suggestion I knelt beside the Master's bed and prayed. In no way deterred by her advanced age or by any physical infirmity, she followed suit. With wonderful spirit and in a most moving manner she recited the Tablet of Aḥmad.

It was only after difficult and prolonged negotiations with the owners and the direct intervention of the Israeli authorities that Shoghi Effendi was able to acquire the land he wanted at the very head of Mount Carmel for the Mashriqu'l-Adhkár of the Holy Land. On the day the purchase was made, someone knocked on Milly's door and told her that the Guardian was waiting for her in his car.[299] Although their conversation as they drove to the site is not recorded, they must have enjoyed this precious experience.

In his message of April 1955 the Guardian informed the 'delegates assembled at the twelve Annual Conventions, convened simultaneously throughout the Bahá'í world during the Riḍván Festival' that 'an area of thirty-six thousand square metres' had been acquired, 'situated on the promontory of Mt Carmel', 'for the price of one hundred and eight thousand dollars, to serve as the site for the first Mashriqu'l-Adhkár of the Holy Land, the entire sum having been donated by Amelia Collins, Hand of the Cause and outstanding benefactress of the Faith'.[300] Further, largely through Milly's 'liberal' contributions, 14 national Ḥaẓíratu'l-Quds had been purchased at a cost of over $200,000. She had also contributed the sum of $50,000, 'as yet another evidence of her munificence', to establish Bahá'í national endowments in 50 countries in five continents.[301]

Both Rúḥíyyih Khánum and Mr Faizi have confirmed that Milly became one of the Guardian's few intimate companions and was often the recipient of his confidence.[302] Mr Faizi recalls Milly telling him that

. . . one night [the Guardian] came to her room with Rúḥíyyih Khánum and explained to her the infamous acts of his relatives. Milly could not bear to see the distress and sorrow in his beautiful face. She was heartbroken and could not suppress her tears. The Guardian, with the greatest tenderness, told her not to weep.[303]

In his Riḍván message of 1957 – the last one he was to write – Shoghi Effendi reviewed the 'superb feats already accomplished . . . by the heroic band of the warriors of Bahá'u'lláh' and stressed the importance of erecting the 'Mother-Temples of the European, the Australian and African continents', remarking that Milly had contributed over a hundred thousand dollars towards these projects.[304]

On the day he left Haifa to spend several months in Europe, in June of that same year, Shoghi Effendi took Milly's hand in his and looked deep into her eyes. 'Don't be sad, Milly,' he said.[305]

When Shoghi Effendi had first asked Milly to come to the Holy Land he had told her it was her 'home'. With his approval, however, she spent each summer in the United States to receive treatment for her arthritis and to attend to personal business. Shortly after the Guardian left Haifa Milly went to Arizona for several months, hoping that its hot, dry climate would ease the severe pain she suffered. While she was in Arizona the Guardian wrote his final letter to the Bahá'í world, in October 1957.

He called for five intercontinental conferences to be held successively in Kampala, Sydney, Frankfurt, Chicago and Djakarta in January, March, May, July and December 1958. Five Hands of the Cause, 'who, in their capacity as members of the International Bahá'í Council' were 'closely associated with the rise and development of the institutions of the Faith at its World Centre', were chosen to act as his 'special representatives'. Milly was to represent him in Frankfurt.[306]

Anxious to greet the Guardian and Rúḥíyyih Khánum on their return to the Holy Land, Milly left the United States a few days before they were expected home, arriving in Haifa on Sunday 3 November. About 24 hours later she heard the heart-breaking news of the Guardian's death in London.

The next morning, despite her advanced aged, frail health and abounding grief, and carrying petals from the threshold of the Shrine of the Báb, Milly flew to London.[307] From the time of her arrival that evening throughout the subsequent days of agony, Milly gave Rúḥíyyih Khánum 'much-needed, warm, motherly love and support'.[308]

On Thursday afternoon, 7 November, as the body of the Guardian, with only the face unshrouded, lay in its coffin, Rúḥíyyih Khánum 'spread over that treasured form, covering it from feet to chin', like a 'sacred carpet of love', the rose petals that Milly had brought from Haifa.[309]

Early the next evening Rúḥíyyih Khánum and Milly drove from their hotel to the Great Northern London Cemetery near Barnet to inspect the grave that had been prepared for the beloved Guardian's remains and to see the chapel where the funeral service was to be held. Later that same evening they joined the other eleven Hands of the Cause now in London to arrange with them a programme of befitting prayers and meditations.

The next morning, Saturday 9 November, at 10:40, Rúḥíyyih Khánum and Milly, followed by a funeral cortège of over 360 believers in more than 60 automobiles, departed for the cemetery from the British Ḥaẓíratu'l-Quds at 27 Rutland Gate, close to Hyde Park in London, and journeyed to the place where the hearse carrying the body of the Guardian stood. Headed by a floral hearse, the funeral cortège made its way to the cemetery in less than an hour.[310]

The chapel was so full that more than a third of the friends had to stand outdoors or in the aisle. Milly sat beside Rúḥíyyih Khánum to the right of the casket with the Hands of the Cause immediately behind them.[311]

Rúḥíyyih Khánum recounts:

All stood while the wonderful prayer, ordained by Bahá'u'lláh for the dead, was chanted in Arabic. Six other prayers and excerpts from the Teachings were then read by friends with beautiful voices, some in English, some in Persian . . . In solemn file the friends followed the casket as it was borne out, placed in the hearse again, and slowly driven the few hundred yards to the graveside . . . As all stood, silently waiting for the coffin to be lowered into the grave, Rúḥíyyih Khánum felt the agony of the hearts around her penetrate into her own grief. He was their Guardian. He was going forever from their eyes, suddenly snatched from them by the immutable decree of God, Whose Will no man dare question.[312]

Rúḥíyyih Khánum and Milly returned to Haifa. On Friday 15 November, in the company of Mason Remey, Leroy Ioas, Ugo Giachery and Milly, Rúḥíyyih Khánum entered the Guardian's apartment and sealed with wax his safe and desk. Hand of the Cause Paul Haney relates:

Three days later, on November 18, 1957, just two weeks after the ascension of the Guardian, the Hands of the Cause assembled in the Holy Land, held a memorial meeting in the precincts of the Shrine of Bahá'u'lláh, and entered upon those fateful days of prayerful and soul-searching consultation which led to the vital and far-reaching decisions arrived at during the course of this first Conclave of the Hands.[313]

Milly was among the nine Hands of the Cause who the next morning broke the seals that had been placed on the Guardian's safe and examined with great care its contents.

After a thorough search the nine Hands signed a document testifying that no Will or Testament of any nature whatsoever executed by Shoghi Effendi had been found. This information was then reported to the entire body of the Hands assembled in the Mansion of Bahá'u'lláh in Bahjí, adjoining His tomb.[314]

From its Conclave the Hands of the Cause issued an important resolution and proclamation:

And whereas in accordance with the Will and Testament of 'Abdu'l-Bahá 'the Hands of the Cause must elect from among their own number nine persons that shall at all times be occupied in the important services in the work of the Guardian of the Cause of God';

We nominate and appoint from our own number to act on our behalf as the Custodians of the Bahá'í World Faith

Rúḥíyyih Rabbani
Charles Mason Remey
Amelia E. Collins
Leroy C. Ioas
Ḥasan Balyuzi
'Alí Akbar Furútan
Jalál Kházeh
Paul E. Haney
Adelbert Mühlschlegel

to exercise – subject to such directions and decisions as may be given from time to time by us as the Chief Stewards of the Bahá'í World Faith – all such functions, rights and powers in succession to the Guardian of the Bahá'í Faith, His Eminence the late Shoghi Effendi Rabbani, as are necessary to serve the interests of the Bahá'í World Faith, and this until such time as the Universal House of Justice, upon being duly established and elected in conformity with the Sacred Writings of Bahá'u'lláh and the Will and Testament of 'Abdu'l-Bahá, may otherwise determine.[315]

Milly was now 84 years old, physically frail and in severe pain from arthritis. Nevertheless, she still found the strength to fulfil her ever-present duties, not only in the Holy Land but in many parts of the planet.

As directed by the Guardian, Milly attended the Intercontinental Conference in Frankfurt held from 25 to 29 July 1958. As his representative she opened the conference, attended by almost 2,300 believers, with a moving tribute to him:

We are all, in a way, Shoghi Effendi's heirs. We have inherited his work. His plan is completely laid out. Ours is the task to fulfil it. We must, each of us, complete our share of

the World Crusade. This is the memorial we must build to
our beloved Shoghi Effendi.

Let us love him more now than ever before, and through
the power of our love attract his love to us, and bring his
blessing on our labours.

Let us not fail him, for he never failed us. Let us never
forget him, for he never forgot us.[316]

Milly then read to those assembled the powerful message of
the Hands of the Cause in the Holy Land.

On the third day of the conference, its mid-point, Milly
anointed the friends with attar of roses as, over a period of
four hours, each believer in succession looked at the precious
gifts sent by the Guardian: 'a portion of the blessed earth
from the inmost Shrine of Bahá'u'lláh, a lock of His precious
Hair, and a reproduction of His Portrait'.[317]

During the last two days of the conference a large sum of
money was raised for the erection of the Temple in Frankfurt
and 133 believers volunteered to pioneer.

Milly closed the conference with these words:

> To win one smile from the Guardian is enough to take you
> through a whole year of pioneering, and I am sure that you
> won the first smile today.[318]

In November 1960 the Hands of the Cause announced,
'Amelia Collins will lay the cornerstone of the Mother Temple of Europe during this present month in Frankfurt.'[319] In
her opening remarks at the impressive ceremony, Milly said:

> Our beloved Guardian in his infinite wisdom chose the very
> heart of Europe as the site for this temple. It will be the fifth
> Mashriqu'l-Adhkár to be erected by the Bahá'ís of the
> world, and from it will stream forth special grace and
> blessing upon this continent, the cradle of western civiliza-
> tion, so war-torn, so in need at this time of the spiritualizing
> forces latent in the teachings of the Manifestation of God
> for this day . . . This Mother Temple of Europe is not only
> unique, but is distinguished by the fact that the beloved
> Guardian himself specified it should receive the infinitely

precious gift of some of the sacred dust from the Shrine of
Bahá'u'lláh. In 1958, at the time of the Intercontinental
Conference in Frankfurt . . . I delivered this dust to the
German National Assembly for safe-keeping, little dreaming
it would ever be my joy and privilege to place this gift in the
foundation of this glorious Temple.
I now do so in the name of our most beloved Shoghi
Effendi.[320]

Hand of the Cause Mr Faizi has given us a vivid description
of Milly as she was after the passing of Shoghi Effendi.
Despite the steadily increasing pain arising from her arthritis, she always attended the meeting of the Hands. 'Her
presence was a great help,' Mr Faizi writes. 'Every word she
uttered welled up from a fountain-head of love deep in her
pure heart. Her eyes grew wider, bluer and more penetrating
when ways and means were found to open up paths towards
the fulfilment of one of the goals of the Guardian's Ten Year
Plan.'[321]

After the passing of Shoghi Effendi Milly tried to be with
Rúḥíyyih Khánum as often as possible during her 'bitter
hours of loneliness and separation'. Whenever Rúḥíyyih
Khánum went on a journey Milly would encourage her
gently, 'Rest assured, my darling. Rest assured that wherever
you go, Shoghi Effendi will be standing next to you, and
whatever step you take, he will hold your hand and will guide
your steps.'[322]

During the autumn of 1961, after resting in Arizona for
some weeks, Milly visited her old home in Wilmette. There
she fell downstairs and fractured her arm. Despite this, she
shortly afterwards travelled to Haifa to arrive in time for the
opening of the fifth Conclave of the Hands. In acute pain,
unable to walk properly and needing some of the friends to
aid her up the stairs of the Master's House, Milly's face
'shone with the light of love'.[323]

During the last years of His life, Bahá'u'lláh resided in the
Mansion at Bahjí. It was in this House that the Hands gathered in November 1961 to make decisions regarding the

forthcoming election of the Universal House of Justice. Illness prevented Milly from attending any of the sessions of the Conclave but this all-important one; some of the friends carried her in a chair up the stairs to the central hall. She spoke with 'great conviction and strength, showering her abounding love upon all her co-workers'.[324]

When the meeting was over, the Hands visited the Shrine of Bahá'u'lláh, where Milly read a prayer, 'every word of which took wings to the Abhá Kingdom'.[325]

Back in the Master's house, Milly was confined to bed. Although her doctor would not permit lengthy visits, some of the Hands were allowed to sit at her bedside for just a few minutes at a time to tell her of the decisions they had reached and the progress of the Cause. Sitting up in bed, Milly carefully read and then signed each letter sent by the Hands. The last letter brought to her was about the deputization fund. 'With trembling and aching fingers she held the pen and wrote "Am . . ." and could do no more.'[326]

Mr Faizi had often chanted poems and Tablets for Milly in Persian, translating them into English afterwards. At their last meeting she asked him to do so again. He chanted a prayer of the Master, in which we are asked to 'open our eyes and behold the grandeur and beauty of the Abhá Kingdom . . . When man's soul spreads its wings and gets ready for the eternal flight, he sees some signs of the majesty of God's creation and the immensity of the world beyond'.[327]

During the last weeks of Milly's life Rúḥíyyih Khánum was always with her. On the last day of her life Milly saw to the needs of a pioneer in North America.[328] On the afternoon of 1 January 1962, Milly died in the arms of Rúḥíyyih Khánum. At midnight Rúḥíyyih Khánum, Mr Faizi and 'Alí Nakhjavání went to Milly's room, where Milly was lying on her bed. Mr Faizi remembers:

A heavenly smile adorned her very beautiful face. All the ailments, distress and suffering had gone. With that lovely

105

smile she was able to tell us more clearly than with any words that she had found her lost beloved.[329]

The next day Milly was buried in the Bahá'í cemetery at the foot of Mount Carmel, near the remains of Hand of the Cause John E. Esslemont and those of Ḥájí Mírzá Vakílu'd-Dawlih, a cousin of the Báb and the chief builder of the Mashriqu'l-Adhkár of Ishqabad. The same day the Hands of the Cause cabled:

> With deepest regret share news Bahá'í World passing dearly loved Hand Cause outstanding benefactress Faith Amelia Collins. Unfailing support, love devotion beloved Guardian darkest period his life brought her unique bounty his deep affection, esteem, confidence and honour direct association work World Centre. Signal services every field Bahá'í activity unforgettable. Purchase site Mashriqu'l-Adhkár Mount Carmel, generous gifts hastening construction Mother Temples four continents and acquisition national Ḥaẓíratu'l-Quds endowments, constant support home front and worldwide teaching enterprises among her magnificent donations. Urge national assemblies hold memorial gatherings, particularly Temples, commemorate her shining example ceaseless services maintained until last breath.[330]

5

Kate Dwyer

On 9 October 1920, Kate Dwyer, the fourth child of Catholic parents, was born in the town of Daylesford, eleven miles from the village of Spargo Creek in the Australian mining province of Victoria. Kate's parents owned the Mineral Springs Hotel in Spargo Creek and lived in it with their children. Mr and Mrs Dwyer ran the hotel, their nearby farm, the local post office and the telephone service.

Kate had three older brothers – Michael, Timothy and Jerimiah – and a brother who was some years younger than herself, John. She and her brothers attended the local state school, walking in all six miles to and from it each day. The school boasted 24 pupils and one master to teach them. Kate's class comprised two boys and herself.

When they were children Kate and her brothers sometimes fought among themselves but as they grew older they stopped even having cross words one with another. Every day they prayed together with their parents and said the rosary. Kate spent her girlhood in an atmosphere of love and warmth. She and her brother Jerimiah, who was two years her senior, became special friends, and Kate can still remember the ache in her heart when he left home for the first time to attend school in Daylesford. Kate also had a close relationship with John and played the important role of 'his little mother'.

Kate's father did not tolerate bad language being spoken in his hotel and those who stayed there knew that their conduct must be above reproach. As young people Kate and her brothers did not always enjoy helping to run their parents' hotel. At one time Kate actually hated to work in it but realizing that her parents needed the money it brought, she prayed for God's help. Without telling anyone how she felt, she made a renewed effort to help them.

As soon as Kate and her brothers reached the age of 14, their parents sent them in turn to a school in Daylesford to receive their secondary education. While she was attending this school Kate boarded with the Presentation nuns at the Holy Cross Convent. It soon became apparent, however, that owing to her mother's frail health, Kate was needed to help again in the hotel. She returned home before completing the first year of her secondary education.

Although Kate was not much interested in music, for the next two years she travelled, at her mother's request, eleven miles by bus each week to the convent for a piano lesson.

When Kate was 14 she first felt the desire to become a nun. Because he mother's health did not improve, however, and knowing how much she, as the only daughter, was needed at home, Kate gave up her intended calling and began to take an enthusiastic part in the social life of the village. Greatly enjoying dances and supper parties, she made many friends among the boys. The liberty her parents allowed her made her the envy of the other girls in the neighbourhood. During her free time Kate raised funds, mostly for the church but also for the football, tennis and cricket clubs.

Despite the happy life she led, Kate felt she could not attain true fulfilment except in service to God within the church. Her keenly perceptive mother realized this. Although she had dreams of a successful marriage for Kate, Mrs Dwyer did not stand in her daughter's way. As Kate has written:

> I loved all life had to offer, and was secure within a happy family circle, but I felt that God was calling me to something higher and that I must follow that call. There was little about the life that I was contemplating that attracted me.

I would dearly have loved to be married and have children, but I felt that only in the convent would I find that inner contentment and fulfilment to which I felt drawn.[331]

Much to the amazement of her friends, all of whom knew that she greatly enjoyed her life at home, Kate, at the age of 19, entered the convent. It was September 1939, just after the outbreak of the second world war.

On the day that Kate left home her parents and all her brothers, except Michael, cried. Kate remembers, 'Mick seemed to understand more fully the great privilege that was mine, and through me, our family's also. He seemed to be in another world.'[332]

The Presentation nuns, who Kate already knew and loved, were primarily teachers. Kate could not see herself as a teacher, wanting rather to help people with serious problems. She decided to join the Sisters of St Joseph, who did a great deal of social welfare work. After completing her training as a novice, Kate was sent to a girls' hostel. Deeply interested in young people, she found the work assigned to her very rewarding. She stayed in the hostel for 16 years and still maintains warm relationships with some of the women she had known there as girls.

When Kate entered the convent in 1939 nuns were trained to give their families little thought. Obedient to these instructions, Kate seldom saw hers, which caused her family much grief. Years later, after several strokes had confined Mrs Dwyer to a wheelchair for seven years, Kate saw her mother again. In January 1952 Kate happened to be taking a holiday in a neighbouring convent and went to visit her mother. While there, Mrs Dwyer died, her head in Kate's arms. Three years later Kate's father had a stroke. Kate was able to visit him only twice before he too passed away.

In 1963 Kate moved to a maternity home in Carlton, an inner city suburb of Melbourne. The main task of the nuns was to take care of the unmarried mothers and their babies. She and the other nuns often gave advice both to the girl and boy concerned. Sometimes only the girl herself knew she was pregnant; at other times it was the father of the child who needed support and guidance. Some girls, although usually deeply grieved at the prospect, felt compelled to give their babies up for adoption.

The order to which Kate belonged was not a hierarchical one, the nun holding the position of Mother Superior being referred to as Sister-in-Charge. In 1969 Kate was appointed to this office.

Kate could tell many stories of her life in the convent. In 1970, for example, a lonely girl whose family had turned her out of their home brought her baby to the convent on Christmas Day, as she had nowhere else to go. The nuns greeted the girl and her child warmly and insisted that they spend the day with the nuns. Although Kate could tell many such stories, those who came there for help knew that the nuns would never betray a confidence. It was understood that even should a nun someday meet one of the girls face-to-face, the nun would pretend not to know the girl, unless the girl spoke first.

Kate loved her life in the convent. Entirely fulfilled in her service to Christ, she had never given much consideration to the possibility that He would return. Absorbed in her work as a nun, she was not conscious of making any further search for spiritual truth.

Although physically strong, Kate suffered from asthma. In the spring of 1971, hoping that chiropractic treatment might at least alleviate her condition, she began to make regular visits to a clinic run by Frank and Maryann McLeod. The McLeods were Bahá'ís. Kate did not know this, not being interested in their religious affiliation.

Kate had been attending the clinic for about two months when the McLeods decided to convert part of their waiting room into a Bahá'í bookshop with a separate entrance. One afternoon when Kate arrived for her treatment she saw in the window of the clinic a poster reading 'Bahá'í Unites Mankind'. In idle curiosity, Kate went into the bookshop to find out how to pronounce the world 'Bahá'í' and what it meant. The woman looking after the bookshop was also the receptionist in the clinic and knew nothing about the Bahá'í Faith. Not wanting to spend the cost of a book, Kate asked the receptionist for a small pamphlet. The receptionist handed her one with an attractive cover, commenting, 'This is a nice pamphlet.'

The pamphlet was *A Flame of Fire*, Hand of the Cause A. Q. Faizi's moving and vivid account of the story of the Tablet of Aḥmad – perhaps not the best choice for someone with no knowledge at all of the Bahá'í teachings. No doubt a Bahá'í would have chosen a different introductory pamphlet for Kate.

The pamphlet tells the story of Aḥmad, born in Persia around 1805, who at an early age is attracted to the mystical path and wants 'to find new paths to truth'.[333] To look on the face of the Qá'im, the Promised One of Islam, becomes his most passionate desire. When he is about 20, he leaves his father's home to search for the Promised One. He wanders from village to village, listening to all the spiritual leaders he meets, but finds no assistance to his search. He travels to Bombay, where he practises the ascetic life, but still finds himself 'in darkness'.[334] He returns to Persia, where he marries and works, still unable to find the goal of his quest. One day he asks a traveller whether a rumour that the Promised One is near is true. The traveller advises him to go to Mashhad and ask for Mullá 'Abdu'l-Klalíq. Aḥmad takes this advice, walking the whole five hundred miles. 'Abdu'l-Klalíq, realizing that Aḥmad is sincere in his search, takes him to meet a follower of the Báb. Aḥmad, learning of the Faith of the Báb, embraces it with all his heart. On returning home, he meets another follower of the Báb, who has persuaded the guards taking the Báb from Isfahan to Tehran to let the Báb stay in his house for a few nights. Aḥmad himself is thus able to meet the Báb and is struck by His 'meekness, grandeur and majesty'.[335] Shortly after, so many people in his town become followers of the Báb that the authorities are alarmed and persecutions begin. Aḥmad hides in a tower for 40 days. Eventually Aḥmad leaves for Baghdad, where the one promised by the Báb has been residing. Aḥmad is overwhelmed when he meets Bahá'u'lláh. Aḥmad makes his residence in Baghdad, working as a hand-weaver. When Bahá'u'lláh is to leave Baghdad Aḥmad begs to go with Him, but Bahá'u'lláh instructs him to remain behind. After some time Aḥmad follows Bahá'u'lláh to Constantinople, only to discover that Bahá'u'lláh has gone to Adrianople. However, Bahá'u'lláh sends a Tablet of particular potency and significance to Aḥmad, which he reads 'again and again'. Aḥmad realizes that he is not to go to Adrianople but to return to Persia to teach the Cause of Bahá'u'lláh. He spends the rest of his long life travelling across Persia telling all he meets of the Cause of Bahá'u'lláh.

When Kate went home to the convent that afternoon she began to read this story. At first she thought it was ridiculous and nearly threw the pamphlet into the fire. Instead, she put it into a drawer. The next day she kept thinking about it and concluded that the McLeods would not distribute the pam-phlet if its contents were 'weird and dreadful'.[336] She took the pamphlet out of the drawer and reread it with much care. She realized that in order to understand the story she would have to learn something about its background.

Kate thought she was investigating the Bahá'í Faith merely out of curiosity. Over a period of weeks she read some Bahá'í books and discussed them with the McLeods. As she contin-ued to study the teachings, her desire for further information increased and she became more and more convinced that what Bahá'u'lláh had revealed was true. When she first began to agree with what she was reading, Kate became very much disturbed. When she realized that the Bahá'í teachings were influencing her life, she consulted with her spiritual director and various priests. Initially they advised her that these teachings could do no harm, but eventually they told her that the teachings were erroneous. As her spiritual mentors were only able to give Kate answers based on the teachings of the

Catholic Church – answers Kate herself already knew – she conferred with them less and less often during her spiritual search. Kate remembers:

> I was in a very comfortable situation in the convent. I had never had any doubts about my calling. I loved the Church and had great respect for it. I was a forward-thinking person and was always happy with the changes that were taking place in the Church, but I was never pushing for them.[337]

Because she was so devoted to the Church, the closer Kate came to accepting the truth of the Bahá'í revelation, the harder she tried to find errors in it so that she could push it away. Daily she asked herself in prayer, 'Was Bahá'u'lláh the Promised One of all ages as He claimed?' Kate's whole life was centred around the Church. She believed implicitly in its doctrines. But Bahá'u'lláh indicated that the Pope, bishops and theologians had misinterpreted the Gospels and were acting much as the scribes and Pharisees had done at the time of Christ.

When Kate read passages such as the following from Bahá'u'lláh's Tablet to Pope Pius IX she must have been greatly shocked:

> Consider those who rejected the Spirit when He came unto them with manifest dominion. How numerous the Pharisees who had secluded themselves in synagogues in His name, lamenting over their separation from Him, and yet when the portals of reunion were flung open and the divine Luminary shone resplendent from the Dayspring of Beauty, they disbelieved in God, the Exalted, the Mighty. They failed to attain His presence, notwithstanding that His advent had been promised them in the Book of Isaiah as well as in the Books of the Prophets and the Messengers. No one from among them turned his face towards the Dayspring of divine bounty except such as were destitute of any power amongst men. And yet, today, every man endowed with power and invested with sovereignty prideth himself on His Name. Moreover, call thou to mind the one

who sentenced Jesus to death. He was the most learned of his age in his own country, whilst he who was only a fisherman believed in Him. Take good heed and be of them that observe the warning.

Consider likewise, how numerous at this time are the monks who have secluded themselves in their churches, calling upon the Spirit, but when He appeared through the power of Truth, they failed to draw nigh unto Him and are numbered with those that have gone far astray. Happy are they that have abandoned them and set their faces towards Him Who is the Desire of all that are in the heavens and all that are on the earth.

They read the Evangel and yet refuse to acknowledge the All-Glorious Lord, notwithstanding that He hath come through the potency of His exalted, His mighty and gracious dominion. We, verily, have come for your sakes, and have borne the misfortunes of the world for your salvation. Flee ye the One Who hath sacrificed His life that ye may be quickened? Fear God, O followers of the Spirit, and walk not in the footsteps of every divine that hath gone far astray . . . Be fair in your judgement and follow not the footsteps of the unjust.[338]

Kate wondered for some time if she would have the courage to stand apart from the church and say, 'I am a Bahá'í'. Fifty-two years old, she found it difficult to believe that God would want her to leave the convent at her age; if she were younger Kate felt she could more easily do so. She worried about the work she was doing for single mothers and their children. If she withdrew from this sphere of activity, who would replace her? The work might go backwards instead of forwards.[339]

Although these thoughts assailed Kate, she steadily became more convinced that Bahá'u'lláh was the Promised One. About eleven months after she had read *A Flame of Fire*, Kate attended her first fireside and met believers other than the McLeods.

It was a rule in Kate's order at that time that nuns never took off their habits except when washing or going to bed.

114

The nuns were, however, permitted to go out with other women who were not nuns. One evening Maryann McLeod called for Kate and took her to the home of Mr and Mrs Payman, a charming Persian couple. Kate recalls, 'Just to enter a Persian home was a big experience for me. All I knew about Persia was Persian carpets. Persian people just didn't come into my train of thought at all.'[340]

Kate sat next to Peter Seery, a young university student. As she described to him her idea of Jesus Christ, she felt sure the others in the room were anxious to know what she was saying. However, no one tried to persuade her of anything, nor did they make her feel she was the centre of attention.

In God Passes By, Shoghi Effendi affirms that the Kitáb-i-Íqán is second only to the Kitáb-i-Aqdas as the 'foremost among the priceless treasures cast forth from the billowing ocean of Bahá'u'lláh's Revelation'.[341] In one passage of this book Bahá'u'lláh explains what every true seeker should do to attain the object of his quest:

> But, O my brother, when a true seeker determineth to take the step of search in the path leading to the knowledge of the Ancient of Days, he must, before all else, cleanse and purify his heart, which is the seat of the revelation of the inner mysteries of God, from the obscuring dust of all acquired knowledge, and the allusions of the embodiments of satanic fancy. He must purge his breast, which is the sanctuary of the abiding love of the Beloved, of every defilement, and sanctify his soul from all that pertaineth to water and clay, from all shadowy and ephemeral attachments. He must so cleanse his heart that no remnant of either love or hate may linger therein, lest that love blindly incline him to error, or that hate repel him away from the truth . . . That seeker must at all times put his trust in God, must renounce the peoples of the earth, detach himself from the world of dust, and cleave unto Him Who is the Lord of Lords. He must never seek to exalt himself above any one, must wash away from the tablet of his heart every trace of pride and vainglory, must cling unto patience and resignation, observe silence, and refrain from idle talk . . .

He should be content with little, and be freed from all inordinate desire . . . At the dawn of every day he should commune with God, and with all his soul persevere in the quest of his Beloved. He should consume every wayward thought with the flame of His loving mention, and, with the swiftness of lightning, pass by all else save Him. He should succour the dispossessed, and never withhold his favour from the destitute. He should show kindness to animals, how much more unto his fellow-man, to him who is endowed with the power of utterance. He should not hesitate to offer up his life for his Beloved, nor allow the censure of the people to turn him away from the Truth. He should not wish for others that which he doth not wish for himself, nor promise that which he doth not fulfil. With all his heart should the seeker avoid fellowship with evil doers, and pray for the remission of their sins. He should forgive the sinful, and never despise his low estate, for none knoweth what his own end shall be . . . Our purpose in revealing these convincing and weighty utterances is to impress upon the seeker that he should regard all else beside God as transient, and count all things save Him, Who is the Object of all adoration, as utter nothingness . . . When the detached wayfarer and sincere seeker hath fulfilled these essential conditions, then and only then can he be called a true seeker . . . Only when the lamp of search, of earnest striving, of longing desire, of passionate devotion, of fervid love, of rapture, and ecstasy, is kindled within the seeker's heart, and the breeze of His loving-kindness is wafted upon his soul, will the darkness of error be dispelled, the mists of doubts and misgivings be dissipated, and the lights of knowledge and certitude envelop his being. At that hour will the mystic Herald, bearing the joyful tidings of the Spirit, shine forth from the City of God resplendent as the morn, and, through the trumpet-blast of knowledge, will awaken the heart, the soul, and the spirit from the slumber of negligence. Then will the manifold favours and outpouring grace of the holy and everlasting Spirit confer such new life upon the seeker that he will find himself endowed with a new eye, a new ear, a new heart, and a new mind. He will contemplate the manifest signs of the universe, and will penetrate the hidden mysteries of the soul. Gazing with the eye of God, he will perceive within every atom a door that leadeth him to the stations of absolute certitude. He will discover in all things the mysteries of divine Revelation and the evidences of an everlasting manifestation. I swear by God! Were he that treadeth the path of guidance and seeketh to scale the heights of righteousness to attain unto this glorious and supreme station, he would inhale at a distance of a thousand leagues the fragrance of God, and would perceive the resplendent morn of a divine Guidance rising above the dayspring of all things. Each and every thing, however small, would be to him a revelation, leading him to his Beloved, the Object of his quest. So great shall be the discernment of this seeker that he will discriminate between truth and falsehood even as he doth distinguish the sun from shadow . . . When the channel of the human soul is cleansed of all worldly and impeding attachments, it will unfailingly perceive the breath of the Beloved across immeasurable distances, and will, led by its perfume, attain and enter the City of Certitude. Therein he will discern the wonders of His ancient wisdom, and will perceive all the hidden teachings from the rustling leaves of the Tree – which flourisheth in that City . . . They that valiantly labour in quest of God's will, when once they have renounced all else but Him, will be so attached and wedded to that City that a moment's separation from it would to them be unthinkable . . . That city is none other than the Word of God revealed in every age and dispensation.[342]

Someone at the fireside read these words to Kate.

That just hit me like a sledge hammer. I knew what I had to do. So I read the Book of Certitude. I didn't need to read it to be convinced, I had reached the stage where I believed that Bahá'u'lláh was the return of Christ. I didn't know a lot about the principles or the laws, but it didn't concern me. If Bahá'u'lláh was the Promised One of all ages, if He was the return of Christ, nothing else mattered. Whatever He said I would have to do.[343]

About two weeks later, on Wednesday 31 May, Kate went to

see the Vicar of Religions, whom she knew well. She told him that not only was she leaving the convent but she was leaving the church as well. After asking her a few questions, the Vicar said to Kate, 'I realize you haven't come for guidance or for direction or counsel. You have simply come to tell me what you are doing.' Kate agreed with him.[344]

Kate asked him what she should do about her vows. Much to her amusement he replied, 'If someone explodes a bomb in Ireland he is hardly going to be booked for a traffic offence.'[345]

Later that evening Kate told her superiors in the convent what she had decided. They instructed her to write to the Holy Father, asking to be released her from vows and giving three reasons for her request. The reasons Kate included in her letter were that she felt that the Holy Spirit was guiding her to leave the church; she no longer believed in all its teachings; and she had accepted the Bahá'í Faith as her way of life. Kate signed three copies of this letter, one intended for the Pope, another for the Bishop and the third for the files of the order. Kate learned some months later that none of these letters left the order's premises.[346]

Kate had not spoken of the Bahá'í Faith to the other nuns while she had been investigating it. As Sister-in-Charge she did not want to confuse them. Further, she was afraid that if her growing interest in the Bahá'í Cause became generally known, her superiors, in their effort to protect her from what they thought was evil, might move her to a convent far from any Bahá'ís.[347] She thought, however, that after she had stated her intention she would have ample time before leaving the convent to explain to the other nuns and to her relatives what she had decided to do.

Kate's superiors found it difficult to believe that she had not yet spoken of the Bahá'í Cause to the other nuns, but realizing that she had not, asked her not to.[348] They also asked her not to communicate with the other nuns after she left the convent. When Kate's superiors learned that Frank and Maryann McLeod had offered Kate hospitality whenever she needed it, they asked Kate to leave the convent immediately. Although much distressed at the little time given her, Kate was anxious to comply with their wishes and arranged for Maryann to collect her four days later. She telephoned her relations to ask whether they needed her but did not tell them of her immediate plans.

On the day of Kate's departure, Sister Juan, the Provincial of Victoria and Kate's counsellor, met with Kate for two hours to decide how they could best break the news to the other sisters. Kate later told the nuns gathered in the community room that she was going away, that this was goodbye, and that Sister Juan would explain all. The impression left was that Kate was being sent to another state. Kate relates, 'I still carry the picture in my mind of their dumbfounded expression. Every one of them loved me as I did them.'³⁴⁹

After Kate had addressed the nuns, Sister Juan took her into a private room and made out a cheque in Kate's name. She hesitated slightly over the amount, then wrote four hundred dollars, a hundred more than was customary to give one leaving the order.³⁵⁰

Kate went directly to her bedroom, took off her habit, kissed for the last time the cross that she had constantly worn since becoming a nun and removed from her finger the ring that the bishop had placed there many years before. 'I laid it gently on the table,' Kate has written. 'I had vowed to God, before the Church and in the hand of the Order, Poverty, Chastity and Obedience, and now Bahá'u'lláh was releasing me from these vows.³⁵¹

At a little before three o'clock that afternoon Kate, bareheaded, wearing a blue frock and clutching a small brown purse with the cheque in it, went down the stairs of the convent for the last time to wait with two of the sisters for Maryann to come. When Maryann arrived with two of her children, Kate and the sisters embraced, tears coursing down their faces.

The sisters said to Maryann, 'Love her, because we love her very much.' Maryann assured them that Kate would be loved and well cared for.[352]

Then Kate turned and, without looking back, walked through the gate and out of the convent.

'That was the day I learned what Divine Providence was all about. I was trusting in a heavenly Father, not knowing what was ahead.'[353]

Kate stayed with the McLeods for two weeks. It was a time of readjustment to a new life. She tells this story about herself.

During her 33 years in the convent Kate had always worn a tight hood over her head, except when she was in bed. When her hair became too long she always clipped it herself, with no concern for how it might look as a result. When she awoke on her first morning away from the convent and looked into the mirror, she saw that her hair was sticking out in all directions. Although she had never been to a hairdresser, she now felt she must do so without delay. At Maryann's suggestion she went to an Italian man. After he had washed her hair, she wondered what he was going to do next. She watched him in the mirror as he picked up one bit of hair after another, dropping each in turn with disdain.

'What is the matter with this hair?' he complained. 'It is terrible!'

'Oh, I've been cutting it myself,' Kate replied. She did not tell him she was just out of the convent, letting him suppose she was Aunty, just down from the bush.[354]

Other problems were shopping and travelling by public transport. The first time Kate went into a supermarket she found it bewildering. It was hard to select goods from the shelf and then wait in line to pay for them. She did not know how to order milk or bread across the counter and worried how she would know their cost. One day a friend offered to drive Kate into the centre of town but Kate refused, saying, 'No, I'll go on the tram. I must get used to it. I must not be dependent on people.' But as she waited at the tram stop in peak hour traffic, she became frightened. She realized that 'people were spending their lives like this'.[355]

Kate's parents and all her brothers but Timothy had died many years earlier. Her widowed sisters-in-law had often turned to Kate for moral support and advice on how to raise their children. Now Kate felt she owed them some explanation of the changes taking place in her life. A few days after leaving the convent she was ready to tell her relatives what she had done. She arranged with Timothy to meet them at his house.

Timothy was shocked by what he heard. Although he loved his sister very much and would do anything for her, her news saddened him. Three of Kate's sisters-in-law thought she was wrong to leave the Church. The fourth, however, expressed her admiration for what Kate had done, and to this day stands up for the Bahá'í Cause when talking to her friends. Two of Kate's nephews later attended a Bahá'í meeting at which Kate spoke about Christianity from a Bahá'í point of view and were favourably impressed.[356]

Kate was sure that she could easily make a living doing the sort of welfare work she had always done in the convent. However, she wished to become independent without delay, so she answered a newspaper advertisement for a female companion and helper for an old woman for six weeks.

Kate's new employer had suffered a stroke and was unable to go out alone. Although a Roman Catholic, the woman made no objection when Kate told her she was a Bahá'í, introducing Kate to her friends as 'my angel who dropped from heaven'. Kate recalls, 'I thought she'd die if she knew where I *had* dropped from!'[357]

The old lady was much disturbed about the state of the Catholic Church, saying to Kate with concern that priests were leaving the priesthood to get married and that nuns were coming out of the convents. The woman did not expect Kate to take her to mass, but to her surprise and pleasure, Kate said she would. Each morning they walked down the street together to arrive in time for the midday service. Kate often took a walk until it was over but sometimes attended the mass. Looking at the service with fresh eyes, Kate did not regret leaving the Church and she became far more secure in new newly-found Faith. She did feel, however, that living with the Catholic woman was a good experience for her.[358] Kate had no difficulty finding a permanent job. For six months she worked as a 'Cottage Mother' in a boys' home in Burwood, a suburb of Melbourne. Some thought it an unusual position for a woman, but Kate told them that the Order of St Joseph ran such homes and that she well knew what working in one of them entailed.[359]

When Kate had left the convent she had been asked not to communicate with any of the nuns. Kate was unhappy about being cut off from her friends but did not contact them. Eventually this ruling was relaxed when the convent officials realized that she was living a normal, peaceful life and was in no way harming the Church. Even while she was looking after 'the dear old lady', Kate received a letter. Dated 16 July 1972, it was written by Sister Juan from St Joseph's Convent:

Dear Catherine,

I was pleased to receive your letter and am pleased too to know that you are well and happy. As Sister Joan has told me, she contacted you, you know that Mother Adrian has taken your place at Carlton. This was a tremendous act on her part to offer her services to us. Sister Josepha from Broadmeadows is looking after the 'girls' and I believe is doing great work.

The day you left, the community was naturally 'thunder-struck' and sad. I stayed there for a week and one good thing came of this, they came to really know me and I them.

Yes, Sister, I pray daily for you and I would say that every Sister in our Order in Victoria does. I have received many letters from our Sisters. All speak in glowing terms of your kindness and inspiration to them, but none can understand how you could give up such lovely persons' companionship – Mary's and Jesus'. Today is the Feast of Our Lady of Mt Carmel. Father told us how Our Lady under the title is the helper of those who wish to communicate with Our Father and her spouse the Holy Spirit, especially in contemplative prayer.

> May God guide you!
> Yours sincerely in J. m J.
> S. M. Juan

About six months later Kate received a second letter from the convent officials, giving her permission to visit the nuns whenever she pleased. Kate was deeply moved by this and immediately resumed her friendships:

> I tell the nuns about activities that are going on, that I am going to a conference or that we have had a convention – but getting down to what I actually believe, I don't talk about it with them. But I would dearly love for them to come and ask me, but they don't, so that's just the way it is.[360]

When Kate left the boys' home she went to Lara, near Geelong, about 40 miles from Melbourne, to work in a girls' home run by the Social Welfare Department. Kate got along very well with the staff and the girls. She would have been happy to remain but after two years she was offered an even more interesting position with Aboriginal Hostels, a government-run company.[361]

Wherever she was and whatever she was doing, after she left the convent Kate had only one object: to teach the Bahá'í Cause. In the spring of 1976 the National Spiritual Assembly of Australia called for pioneers on the home front. Anxious to serve in this capacity, Kate volunteered to move to Mildura, a small town of about 15,000 people on the Murray River about ten hours by train from Melbourne. She found accommodation in the Riverland Motor Inn.

The next March Kate wrote from Mildura to Mother Dennis, the Mother General of the Order of St Joseph:

> Dear Mother Dennis,
>
> As the time of Chapter approaches, I am conscious of the fact that my name may be mentioned for a last time in the

annals of the Order as, probably, a list will be made of those who have left since last Chapter.

Would that you could realize, dear Mother Dennis, the blessing bestowed on the Order, during your term of office, in the fact that Bahá'u'lláh gave me the grace to see the truth of His Revelation and strength to follow Him. Why me, I sometimes wonder; but who are we to question the designs of our loving heavenly Father.

Dear Mother, I pray you may have a share in the deep peace, joy and nearness to God that I have experienced during the last five years. There are those who consider I am deluded, and for them I pray. God is not in competition with Himself, and will gather all His children together, if not in this world then surely in the next.

In beginning this letter, I hoped to convey something of my spiritual happiness, but feel so inadequate to do so. All my life I prayed to be a saint and not to be spared in the making – to be all God wanted me to be. Being human, many times I have drawn back, but the desire was always there. How I longed to identify with Mother Mary in her acquiescence and union with the Will of God. And Mother, as the years of my Bahá'í life go by, my belief in and love for Bahá'u'lláh is reinforced continually. Christ has returned like a thief in the night and is now visible in the Glory of Bahá'u'lláh.

From the above address you will see I am living in Mildura. You may be aware that I held a very good position with a Government Company in Canberra working towards establishing Aboriginal hostels throughout Australia. With the repression of Government spending, the expansion of the Company had ceased and as the goal was for complete Aboriginalization by 1980, I considered my contribution had been made, so I decided to resign, thereby making it possible for another Aboriginal person to move into the Operations Division to which I belonged.

In coming to Mildura, I had no idea what would eventuate for me but once again, as always, Divine Providence has taken care of my material needs. Though offered a position as Field Officer in the Regional office of the Social Welfare Department, I decided I would not again become professionally involved in welfare work, so here I am working three hours a day as a waitress in a cafe – and really enjoying it – and doing part-time receptionist duties in the above motel which I have come to look on as my home for the time being.

Recently, I spent two exciting weeks in New Zealand when, together with ninety-five other Australians, I attended an International Bahá'í Conference in Auckland. It was interesting to visit some of the places I had often heard of from Sister Regina in the past.

Mother, I know you are busy, so I do not expect a reply to my letter, but I did want to be in touch with you at this time, and let you know something of my spiritual and temporal state. Do not be grieved that I am no longer a member of the Order I respect and love so dearly, for God has bestowed a much greater gift on this unworthy soul.

United in the love and service of building God's Kingdom on earth.

With love and gratitude,
Catherine Dwyer

Before coming to Mildura Kate's work put her among people of a type familiar to her and into well-known situations. Now her work as a waitress and receptionist, and later as a dishwasher, opened up a new world to her and she found this a wonderful experience.[362] She continued to teach the Faith and in 1982 wrote:

Most people here know about the Cause of Bahá'u'lláh and have respect for it, but only one local person has joined the Community. Even so we have a Spiritual Assembly.[363]

In 1978 Kate received permission to make a pilgrimage to the Bahá'í World Centre in 1980. She sold her car to obtain the money for the journey, buying a second-hand bicycle to replace it.

On her way to the Holy Land Kate joined Mrs Mahvash Master, a Persian Bahá'í living in Melbourne, travel teaching in Europe for about six weeks.[364] They visited Italy, Austria, Germany, Liechtenstein and Switzerland. Kate's report of this journey appeared in the *Bahá'í International News Service* of 6 June 1981.

The Universal House of Justice suggested to Kate that on her return from the Holy Land she visit Ireland. Kate thought that this might be because of her background. The parents of one young Bahá'í thought the teaching of the Faith to be evil and Kate was asked to talk with them. As she said, 'There can be two results of their meeting with me. Sometimes when Catholics meet me, they stop and wonder and are very pleased to hear my story, but there are others who the moment that they hear a nun has left the convent and become a Bahá'í think that I am bad and oppose the Bahá'í Faith straight off.'[365]

Kate has briefly described this visit to Ireland:

> During my stay in one town a young man devoted several days in gathering his friends in order that I should talk to them. On one occasion, after an exhausting day, I had just returned home when he came in saying, 'I have news for you, Kate, you are going out again', and off we went to meet yet another group of his friends. This boy is an inspiration to all. He has lost a limb in a road accident, yet day after day he would walk the wet and windy streets with me. He is an example of the beautiful Irish Bahá'ís who put Bahá'u'lláh in the centre of their lives and make everything else revolve around the Cause.[366]

While in Ireland Kate spoke at the National Teaching Conference. She affirmed that some people were amazed that she, a nun, had been given the opportunity to investigate the Faith but she believed that this could happen to any nun and that many nuns and priests would make wonderful Bahá'ís. What Kate herself found amazing, she said, was that God had made her spirit so open that she was able to seize the opportunity to investigate the Bahá'í Cause and that God had given her the bounty of belief in Bahá'u'lláh.[367] She told these stories to illustrate her point.

A priest in Spain who knew a Bahá'í was about to hold a

weekend retreat. On his arrival at the appointed place, he found the retreat had been cancelled. Sine he had learned from his Bahá'í friend that during this same weekend a Bahá'í meeting would be taking place in a neighbouring district, and having some spare time on his hands, the priest decided to attend this meeting and so be able to straighten out his friend. Instead, the priest himself got 'straightened out' and soon became a Bahá'í.

A priest in America with whom Kate corresponded had a 'rather horrid time' investigating the Faith. He had been trying both to accept and not accept it for some time. Eventually he began to carry around a declaration card in his pocket. One day, with no intention of signing the card, he said mass and preached his sermon. He then walked down to the altar rails and told his congregation that he would not be performing officially for the Church again. 'Now I am proclaiming my faith in Bahá'u'lláh,' he said, and signed his card.

Kate told the Irish Bahá'ís that society usually treats a person according to his or her position. Australians, for example, are not particularly religious and only ten percent are Roman Catholics. Nevertheless, nuns in Australia are held in fairly high esteem.

> One day just after I had bought my car, I was having diffi-
> culty parking it. I was taking up too much room and a man
> got angry at me because I had some of his space. I couldn't
> help thinking that had this taken place a few weeks earlier
> when I was wearing my habit, he would have given me the
> whole of his space and found nothing too much trouble for
> the Sister. Yet here he is abusing me and telling me off.[368]

When she left Ireland Kate travelled to France, where she visited more than 15 cities. Her apprehension at meeting the French Bahá'í community was dispelled when 'from the moment' of her arrival she was 'enveloped' in its love.[369]

On Kate's return to Mildura in February 1981 the first local spiritual assembly of the town was formed, much to her joy. A month later her brother Timothy's wife suddenly died. Although physically exhausted from her travels, Kate attended the funeral. On the train home she suffered a mild heart attack. She was not ill for long, however, and soon regained her former strength and energy. In September she was well enough to travel to Harcourt, Victoria, to give a radio talk for George Karko on the programme 'New Horizons'.

George asked Kate if she had any regrets about her decision to leave the Church and enter the Bahá'í community. Kate replied:

> How could I have any regrets, George. My whole life was consecrated to Christ, my whole 24 hours of every day . . . Christ said that He would return. Bahá'u'lláh claimed to be the Promised one of all the ages, so for me He had to be the return of Christ. But other people can't see that. I am sorry for them. I respect what they believe and would in no way ever wish to downgrade another person's beliefs, but to me I am now following the greater and more wonderful teachings of the fulfilment of the whole of the New Testament. How could I have any regrets?[370]

In November, just after Kate had begun to feel better than she had in years, Timothy underwent a serious spinal operation. Late that month Kate travelled to Ballarat with the intention of opening his house and spending a few weeks with him. She visited him every day in the hospital and it soon became clear that if he was to return home he would need a permanent housekeeper. Feeling that it was her responsibility to look after him and knowing that the Mildura Assembly could form at Riḍván without her, Kate moved to Ballarat. She stayed with her brother until his death seven years later.

Throughout this time Kate was continually involved in Bahá'í work. She took part in the weekly half-hour Bahá'í radio programme 'The Lote Tree' and helped in the production of radio programmes sponsored by other groups who were interested in bringing about world peace. Like other members of her Bahá'í community, Kate did useful work among the Aborigines and spoke to many of the Bahá'í teachings.[371] Early in 1988 Kate offered her services to the National Aboriginal and Islander Working Group. As a result she was asked to pioneer to Arnhem a large area in the north of Australia.

In February 1989 Kate wrote:

Coming from the extreme cold of Ballarat, Victoria, I wondered how I'd cope with the tropical heat of the north where there are only two seasons, the wet and the dry. But Bahá'u'lláh has blessed me with good health and endurance – if that word can be used in the circumstances – and I have been living very happily since last July.

The teaching work among the Aborigines in this far-flung outpost is very slow as the Christian churches have a great hold on the people here. So it is, as the beloved Guardian stated, 'by our example rather than by our words' that those dear, pure souls will be led to the truth.[372]

Kate Dwyer – who loved and was strongly attached to the Roman Catholic Church, who loved the Order of St Joseph, who held a high position in it – was not deaf to the call of Bahá'u'lláh. When she realized who He was, she gradually turned to Him with all her heart. She longed to help her friends in the convent and the priests attain the same goal. As Bahá'u'lláh revealed:

O concourse of monks! If ye choose to follow Me, I will make you heirs of My Kingdom; and if ye transgress against Me, I will, in My long-suffering, endure it patiently, and I, verily, am the Ever-Forgiving, the All-Merciful.[373]

6

Ella Bailey

Late in 1907 Helen Goodall and her daughter Ella Cooper travelled from California to 'Akká on a pilgrimage to meet 'Abdu'l-Bahá. On their return to Oakland they held weekly meetings in their home to tell people about the Bahá'í Faith. Among those present at these meetings was Ella Bailey, a schoolteacher from Berkeley. She also attended the Nineteen Day Feasts held in Mrs Goodall's home:

> Before we gathered for Feasts each one of us prepared himself with prayers . . . We were met at the door by Helen and Ella [Cooper], their faces illumined with beautiful smiles. We were soon seated at two long tables in the lovely dining room . . . Mrs Goodall asked for a moment of quiet, and we silently said the Greatest Name. Then one of the believers passed from friend to friend anointing our heads with rose perfume and saying, 'As this perfume is to the nostrils, so may this spiritual food refresh the soul.'. . . Each one then read a verse from the *Hidden Words of Bahá'u'lláh*, often followed by a prayer sent by 'Abdu'l-Bahá to Helen.[374]

One evening Ella Bailey, 'truly a blessed soul with a sweet, charming, ready smile', was asked to anoint the friends.[375]

Ella Martha Bailey was born in Houston, Texas, on 18 December 1864. While she was still a baby her parents moved to a ranch in San Diego County, California. When she was two she suffered an attack of polio; as a result, one of her legs was permanently paralysed. Despite this, Ella was very fond of the outdoors and learned to ride horseback expertly.

Ella was a very pretty young woman but decided to remain unmarried so that she could serve the wider community more effectively. As she was interested in the guidance of children, she studied to become a teacher. She took a position in a school in Berkeley, where she moved after leaving normal school in southern California. Ella taught elementary school grades and was very much loved by her pupils.[376]

Early in the century Ella learned of the Bahá'í Faith through Lua Getsinger. The Berkeley home of Dr Woodson Allen and his wife Frances was often the venue for Bahá'í meetings and Lua was frequently invited to spend weekends there to tell others about the Faith. No doubt Ella attended many of these meetings. Ramona Brown recalls that Lua

> . . . liked to sit in corner of the room so that she could look into the face of each person while she spoke. Lua was a lovely portrait in her blue costume. She had pretty brown hair, ivory skin, naturally red lips, and blue eyes which were accentuated by a soft blue scarf falling from her hat across her shoulders. A celestial radiance seemed to surround her as she spoke with a simplicity and charm that attracted many people to the Faith.[377]

Lua's instruction led Ella to accept the Faith. She was thus 'one of the "waiting servants" who embraced the Faith prior to the American visit of 'Abdu'l-Bahá'.[378]

In 1909 Ella received a Tablet from 'Abdu'l-Bahá:

To Ella M. Bailey,
Upon her be Bahá'u'lláh!

He is God!

O thou maidservant of God!

Be thou not sad on account of past vicissitudes and troubles, neither be thou discouraged by hardships and difficulties.

Be thou hopeful in the Bounty of the True One, and be thou happy and rejoiced in the love of God.

This world is the arena of tests, trials, and calamities. All the existing things are targets for the arrows of mortalities; therefore, one must not feel sad or disheartened on account of the travails or become hopeless over the intensity of

132

misfortune and distress.

Praise be to God that thou hast found the guidance of God, hast entered into the Kingdom of God, hast attained to peace and tranquillity, and hast obtained a share from the Everlasting Bounty and Mercy. Therefore, pass the remaining days of thy life with the utmost joy and fragrance; and, with a joyful heart and tranquil mind, live and act under the protection of His Highness, the Clement.

Upon thee be Bahá-Al-Abhá!

Abdul Baha Abbas[380]

In 1910 Ella travelled to the Los Angeles area for a visit. The *Bahá'í News* of 13 July 1910 lists several Bahá'í activities taking place in Los Angeles and its suburbs and reports, 'Miss Ella Bailey of Berkeley visited the friends and is now spending the summer at Banning, California'.[380]

On the morning of 11 April 1912 'Abdu'l-Bahá arrived in New York City at the beginning of His epoch-making journey of nearly eight months throughout the North American continent. Thinking that He might not travel to California, Ella, together with Helen Goodall and Ella Cooper, went to Washington to meet Him and then followed Him to Chicago. The three stayed in the same hotel as 'Abdu'l-Bahá and were able to meet Him privately. One day 'Abdu'l-Bahá sent for them. They had earlier put flowers in His room. Now He said:

You are more to me than the flowers for you are my living flowers. These flowers have only colour, but you have life. It makes me very happy to see you. When the hearts are pure it makes me very happy. This is what we came for – that the hearts might be made pure. I care not for ease, I care not for comfort. When I see pure hearts, then nothing else matters.[381]

Ella recalls:

We wondered what He looked like, the colour of His eyes, of His hair. After I had once seen Him, I never had words

133

with which to express these things. They seemed so unimportant . . . He greeted me by saying that He was happy to see me with my spiritual mother, thereby confirming a beautiful relationship that continued for life between Mrs Goodall and myself.[382]

This meeting also 'sealed the relationship of sister between Miss Bailey and Mrs Cooper'.[383]

At a private meeting with Ella 'Abdu'l-Bahá repeated her name many times:

'Oh, Ella Bailey, Ella Bailey! Oh, Ella Bailey, Ella Bailey! Oh, Ella Bailey! . . .' He kept repeating my name as He looked off into space. But He put into my name every possible emotion. That was the wonder of it.[384]

For Ella, these words conveyed a special meaning: 'My child, you are going to suffer. You are going to have a great deal of pain. Life is going to be hard.'[385] She later remarked:

In those few words He gave me all the emotions of a lifetime. He gave suffering but with it He gave me faith and strength. This made me feel His spiritual power and His truth.[386]

Together with Mrs Goodall and Ella Cooper, Ella attended all the meetings addressed by 'Abdu'l-Bahá in Chicago, including the last session of the fourth annual convention of the Bahá'í Temple Unity at which He dedicated the grounds and laid the foundation stone of the future Mashriqu'l-Adhkár.

On 5 May, the day before He left for Cleveland, 'Abdu'l-Bahá met with the children of the Chicago friends. The two Ellas were there to record the event:

Although many lived [a] considerable distance and found it necessary to arise as early as five o'clock, yet promptly at the appointed hour of eight, about thirty-five children were on hand to greet him and to receive the spiritual baptism in store for them.

They were gathered in a circle in the middle of the

beautiful parlour of The Plaza, the parents and friends making a circle behind them. When 'Abdu'l-Bahá entered all arose. While he took the seat prepared for him, the children sang without accompaniment, 'Softly His Voice is Calling Now'.

. . . He called each child to him in turn, took them in his lap, petting and stroking their hair and hugging and kissing the little ones, pressing the hands and embracing the older ones, all with such infinite love and tenderness shining in his eyes and thrilling in the tones of his voice, that when he whispered in English in their ears to tell him their names, they answered as joyfully and freely as they would a beloved father. To each child he gave a little different touch, patting some on the breast, some on the back and some on the head. He blessed them all.

. . . The children's joy and his own happiness seemed to culminate when one dear little tot ran to him and fairly threw herself into his arms. When he let her go she stood for a second and then suddenly laughed aloud with perfect joy, which found its instant echo in a ripple around the whole circle.

'Abdu'l-Bahá then stood and spoke . . . 'according to the words of Bahá'u'lláh you are the very lamps or candles of the world of humanity, for your hearts are exceedingly pure and your spirits are most delicate . . . My hope for you is that your parents may educate you spiritually, giving you the utmost ethical training. May your education be most perfect so that each one of you may be imbued with all the virtues of the human world . . . I pray for all of you, asking God's aid and confirmation in your behalf.[387]

Ella reported that 'Abdu'l-Bahá then went into Lincoln Park to be photographed with the children.

'Abdu'l-Bahá then expressed a desire to walk alone and strode majestically away, with his hands clasped behind him. He walked over to the noble Lincoln statue nearby and for a few moments stood gazing up at it, making a remarkably impressive and significant picture – the lonely figure of our immortal Lincoln gazing down upon him who is today giving to the world spiritual emancipation.[388]

Ella, Helen Goodall and Ella Cooper reluctantly returned to California. In the following years Ella dedicated herself to the Faith. She was 'constantly teaching by word and even more, by deed, but she preferred to remain in the background'.[389]

In 1919 at the age of 23, Leroy Ioas, the future Hand of the Cause, married Sylvia Kuhlman and moved with her to San Francisco. They became good friends of Ella.[390] Later, in 1932, Leroy was elected to the National Spiritual Assembly of the United States and Canada. He sometimes confided in Ella the difficulties the National Assembly had trying to raise sufficient funds to complete the Temple in Wilmette. On one occasion Ella said to him that she had saved up enough money to pay for her burial expenses but since it did not matter 'if her bones were laid to rest in a potter's field', she would be happy to help. Her friend Dr Robert Gulick remarks, 'Receipts show that she contributed the sum of a thousand dollars to the Temple Fund on two different occasions.'[391]

In 1924 Ella retired from the McKinley School owing to ill health. The principal of the school wrote her a letter of gratitude and appreciation for her services and example:

> I cannot close this letter without telling you again what a precious thing your friendship has been to me and will continue to be, and how we all have been inspired by your courage and faith.[392]

Ella's qualities were much appreciated by the Bahá'ís as well. Bahia Gulick recalls, 'One of Miss Bailey's greatest virtues was her seemingly endless patience. She exhibited this attribute from the time that she arose in the morning and began to put on the shoe specially designed for her lame leg.'[393]

Robert Gulick remembers:

> Her presentation of the message of Bahá'u'lláh was indeed like that of a royal subject giving his most precious possession to his sovereign. Gentleness and sweetness were her

abiding traits . . . Sound in judgement, she never aroused hostility, nor did she compromise on principle.[394]

She expressed her views in a humble way. Not being fanatical she did not alienate people. When an ardent young Bahá'í suggested as a public lecture topic 'Christ is Not Enough', she quietly suggested that such a theme would repel rather than attract. She was the soul of discretion.[395]

Many were her secret sacrifices. She would give sumptuous dinners for friends who were oblivious to the fact that their hostess very often contented herself with tea, toast and perhaps a little soup. Her whole day passed in cheering the brokenhearted, in helping the needy, in visiting the sick, and in refreshing the spirits of the unending stream of guests that came to see her.[396]

A year after Ella's retirement the first Spiritual Assembly of Berkeley was established at Riḍván 1925. Ella was elected its first chairman and served continuously on that body for more than 20 years. She must certainly have played an important role in the organization of the many meetings held by the Assembly. For example, on 18 October 1931 a 'teaching conference combined with a international amity meeting' was held in Berkeley. Many aspects of the teaching work were discussed and a special emphasis given to the training of children, something dear to Ella's heart.[397]

The Berkeley Bahá'ís sponsored monthly 'Amity Meetings', which were reported to be 'doing much toward eliminating race-self-consciousness in their community'.[398] 'During her long residence at the Berkeley Women's City Club', Ella 'used her membership to sponsor many Bahá'í gatherings. Her room became a kind of clinic for the distressed and disconsolate.'[399]

Ella was a member of the Committee for the Training and Teaching of Children. The seven-strong committee's annual report for 1935 reflected Ella's concern for the welfare of children and her interest in promoting the Cause:

In view of the serious problems in our system of education today in preparing children to meet the responsibilities of a new social order which has suddenly begun to take form, Bahá'í parents and teachers may well feel that they have a great opportunity in paving the way. There are many occasions in their regular school routines when Bahá'í children may discuss before their teachers and class mates the underlying principles of the Bahá'í Faith and the plan for world peace, and it should be the primary responsibility of every Bahá'í parent to see that the child has as much knowledge of the Teachings as he is capable of absorbing. Great truths often fall from the lips of children, and the school room and the playground play their parts in shaping the future.[400]

Late in May 1944, in war-torn London, the British Bahá'ís held their annual convention to coincide with the celebration of the hundredth anniversary of the Declaration of the Báb. Here they initiated a six year teaching plan to take the Bahá'í Faith to all parts of the British Isles. The Guardian responded to their cable:

WELCOME SPONTANEOUS DECISION ADVISE FORMATION NINE-TEEN SPIRITUAL ASSEMBLIES SPREAD OVER ENGLAND WALES SCOTLAND NORTHERN IRELAND AND EIRE PRAYING SIGNAL VICTORY.[401]

This plan was successfully completed in April 1950 with an increase of local assemblies from four to 24. Delighted with this accomplishment, Shoghi Effendi cabled the British Bahá'ís gathered at the convention of 1950 that they stood on the threshold of an even larger undertaking:

HOUR PROPITIOUS GALVANISED FIRMLY KNIT BODY BELIEVERS BRACE ITSELF EMBARK AFTER ONE YEAR RESPITE YET ANOTHER HISTORIC UNDERTAKING MARKING FORMAL INAUGURATION TWO YEAR PLAN CONSTITUTING PRELUDE INITIATION SYSTEM-ATIC CAMPAIGN DESIGNED CARRY TORCH FAITH TERRITORIES DARK CONTINENT WHOSE NORTHERN SOUTHERN FRINGES WERE SUCCESSIVELY ILLUMINATED COURSE MINISTRIES BAHÁ'U'LLÁH 'ABDU'L-BAHÁ. HOUR STRUCK UNDERTAKE

PRELIMINARY STEPS IMPLANT BANNER FAITH AMIDST AFRICAN
TRIBES MENTIONED TABLET CENTRE COVENANT SIGNALISING
ASSOCIATION VICTORIOUS BRITISH BAHÁ'Í COMMUNITY WITH
SISTER COMMUNITIES UNITED STATES EGYPT DESIGNED LAY
STRUCTURAL BASIS BAHÁ'Í ADMINISTRATIVE ORDER SCALE
COMPARABLE FOUNDATION ALREADY ESTABLISHED NORTH
SOUTH AMERICAN EUROPEAN AUSTRALIAN CONTINENTS.

The five countries assigned to assist in the two-year Campaign succeeded in opening 16 new territories on the African continent to the Faith and established 17 local assemblies, among them one in Libya.

The Two Year Plan was itself but a prelude to an even more ambitious undertaking. On 8 October 1952 Shoghi Effendi announced the 'projected launching on the occasion of the convocation of the approaching Intercontinental Conferences on the four continents of the globe the fate-laden, soul-stirring, decade-long, world-embracing Spiritual Crusade',[402] a plan, Shoghi Effendi later explained in his letter of 29 April 1953, 'designed to diffuse the light of God's revelation over the surface of the entire planet'.[403]

The African Intercontinental Teaching Conference took place in Kampala, Uganda, from 12 to 18 February 1953. In his message to the conference Shoghi Effendi called for the consolidation of the 24 territories opened to the Faith in the Africa Campaign, among them Libya.[404]

Encouraged by the Guardian and with the prospect of securing good positions in the foreign aid administration, Ella's friends Bahia and Robert Gulick immediately set about making plans to settle in Tripoli.

Tripoli and Benghazi, both of which lie on the shore of the Mediterranean, were the joint capitals of Libya and between them housed nearly a third of the country's population. In 1953 a few Bahá'ís lived in Tripoli but the city did not have an assembly.

Ella badly wanted to go to Tripoli with her friends but she was too humble to make the suggestion. Sensing this, the Gulicks told her that they would enjoy having her with them.

At first she 'beamed gratefully' at their invitation but 'then a cloud came over her face and she replied, "It would be selfish of me to go to Africa and be a burden."' The Gulicks, however, thought that her presence would be a blessing but to ensure they were doing the right thing, they sent a cable to the Guardian. His reply came at once: 'Approve Bailey accompany you.'[405]

Ella had planned to attend the Jubilee commemoration in Wilmette. After much prayer, it was decided that even with the impending journey to Africa she should still go to the conference at which the American House of Worship was to be dedicated. While in Wilmette Ella attended the main events of the Jubilee, including the dedication of the Temple, and the International Teaching Conference. It was at this conference that Ella confirmed her decision to travel to Libya as a pioneer.[406]

Ella returned to Berkeley 'in excellent spirits and relatively good health'. A friend remarked that her voice had not been so 'light and gay' in 40 years.[407] However, a few days after her return she was struck down by pneumonia and had to move from her home at the Berkeley's Women's City Club to a nursing home. She gradually regained some of her strength and by the summer seemed fit enough to travel. Ella and the Gulicks made their final plans to leave. Old friends warned her such a move would shorten her life but Ella answered, 'I do not find it such a great sacrifice to give up living in a rest home.'[408]

On 14 July 1953 Ella flew from California to New York with the Gulicks and their two-year-old son, Robert. She stayed in the apartment of Dr Fazly Melany, the treasurer of the New York Spiritual Assembly, and was visited by two Hands of the Cause, Dhikru'lláh Khádem and Músa Banání. While in New York she had a bad fall but was still able to fly on to Rome as planned. Here she sustained another fall and the stay in Italy had to be cut short. Supplied with an oxygen mask, Ella, together with the Gulicks, flew to Libya and arrived in Tripoli on 20 July, where two Bahá'ís met them at the airport.

Ella did not fully recover her health. Additional falls in Tripoli weakened her further and she was sometimes unaware of her condition. Whenever she did realize her infirmities she profusely thanked Bahia's mother, Mrs Shawat-'Alí Faraju'lláh, for taking care of her and apologized for being such a burden. She enjoyed the visits of the Gulick's small son, whom she loved deeply.

Ella's condition steadily worsened and eventually she had to be transferred to the government hospital. She was visited by a number of Bahá'ís, including a former member of the National Spiritual Assembly of Egypt and the Sudan, Mustapha Effendi Salem; and Mohsen Inayat, who later became a well-known international lawyer and whose great-aunt was Munírih Khánum, the wife of 'Abdu'l-Bahá.[409]

Ella died at twilight at eight o'clock on 26 August 1953. She was 88 years old. Many Bahá'ís gathered at her bedside to read prayers in Arabic and English:

> It was a touching demonstration of international Bahá'í solidarity, of uncalculated affection in an age of calculated risks. Particularly memorable was the moving scene in which an Egyptian friend kissed her forehead and tearfully bade her farewell, 'Goodbye, Miss Bailey'.[410]

The next day a funeral service was held at the Government Cemetery outside Tripoli. That evening Ella's casket was placed in a niche in the cemetery wall. A few days later the American National Assembly prayed for her at the recently-dedicated Wilmette Temple.

The Guardian cabled the friends in Tripoli, 'Grieve at passing of valiant exemplary pioneer. Reward in Kingdom bountiful'[411] and put a gold star on one of his maps to mark the place of her passing.[412] He asked three of the Americans in Tripoli – Robert and Bahia Gulick and Laura Allen[413] – to design a fitting memorial for her grave. Shoghi Effendi himself bore the cost of the gravestone.[414]

Shoghi Effendi included in his cablegram to the Intercontinental Teaching Conference held in New Delhi at the close of the Holy Year in October 1953 a tribute to Ella:

> Irresistibly unfolding crusade sanctified death heroic eighty eight year old Ella Bailey elevating her rank martyrs Faith shedding further lustre American Bahá'í community consecrating soil fast awakening African continent.[415]

Although Ella never wrote to the Guardian – her humility prevented her from doing so – and she never met him, yet 'he perceived the inner worth and true greatness of this wonderful lady'.[416] He ranked her among the 'distinguished band of her co-workers in the Abhá Kingdom' – Martha Root, Lua Getsinger, May Maxwell, Hyde Dunn, Susan Moody, Keith Ransom-Kehler, Dorothy Baker and Marion Jack – 'whose remains, lying in such widely scattered areas of the globe as Honolulu, Cairo, Buenos Aires, Sydney, Tihran, Isfahan, Tripoli and the depths of the Mediterranean Sea attest the magnificence of the pioneer services rendered by the North American Bahá'í Community in the Apostolic and Formative Ages of the Bahá'í Dispensation'.[417]

7

Ella Quant

Ella Quant patiently stood on the New York pier early in the morning of 11 April 1912 and watched as a huge ship broke through the fog and mist. She, like so many of the others gathered on the pier, was awaiting the arrival of 'Abdu'l-Bahá who was about to begin His eight-month journey through North America. As the ship docked, 'subdued excitement, glorious anticipation at the joy of meeting the Master, filled the hearts and radiated from the faces and voices of the friends'.[418] Soon word came from 'Abdu'l-Bahá: He would meet them all at the home of Mr and Mrs Kinney later in the day. The Bahá'ís began to drift away, but Ella and her friend Margaret La Grange did not leave: 'knowing that 'Abdu'l-Bahá was on the vessel', we 'could not tear ourselves away from the pier; so, lingering, our eyes riveted, we were rewarded with a glimpse of Him for whom our hearts longed. Then, satisfied, in anticipation of the afternoon meeting, we, too, left the pier.'[419]

Little is known of Ella Quant's life before she first learned of the Bahá'í Faith in 1903; even her birth date is unknown. She never married. She is listed in 'The History of the Johnstown Assembly' as having become a Bahá'í in 1903.[420] Her teachers were Isabella and James Brittingham.

The Brittinghams had heard the Bahá'í message early in 1898 and had become Bahá'ís shortly afterwards. In October 1900 they moved from New York City to Johnstown, a town about four miles north of the Mohawk River and about 50 miles west of Albany in the state of New York. Shortly after they had settled in, two teachers sent to America by 'Abdu'l-

Bahá arrived in New York City. The Brittinghams requested that they visit Johnstown to give the 'Bread of Life'. Thus Ḥájí Mírzá Ḥasan-i-Khurásání and Mírzá Asadu'lláh, along with their interpreter Mírzá Ḥusayn Rúḥí, travelled to Johnstown in November 1900 where they taught the Faith for two days. This gave impetus to the teaching work in the town and over the course of the next three and a half years about a dozen people became Bahá'ís.

The first community meeting of the Johnstown Bahá'ís took place in January 1902 at the Brittingham's home. Rules for all future meetings were drawn up and adopted:

> That a regular meeting for worship and communion be held once a week . . . that the meetings shall be conducted by the member in whose home it is held . . . It shall be opened at eight o'clock by the Greatest Name spoken in greeting to which all will respond with the same. Then each member in turn shall read a Tablet of some Holy Utterances of the Blessed Perfection or of the Master, 'Abdu'l-Bahá.
>
> Any communication connected with the Faith will then be read or reported. The usual length of the meeting is to be three quarters of an hour, and to be closed by the member who is leading it . . . after which all will silently use the Greatest Name nine times . . . It was decided that not any words save the Words of the Kingdom should be spoken during these evenings.[421]

The community received its first Tablet from 'Abdu'l-Bahá in June 1902. It was translated into English on 24 June:

> O ye brilliant Realities!
> Blessed are ye for that ye believed in the Lord of Hosts, advanced unto the Kingdom of God with faces rejoicing with the Glad Tidings of God . . . Thank your Lord for making ye signs of guidance, and standards of the Supreme Kingdom. Be not sorrowful on account of the affliction of 'Abdu'l-Bahá, for calamity is a light whereby His face glistens among the Supreme Concourse; affliction is healing to His breast, joy to His heart, happiness to His soul; nay, rather, a most honoured garment upon His temple, best

gown upon His body, and dearest crown on His head. This is His utmost desire . . .[422]

Thornton Chase visited the community in December 1902. Fred Ackerknecht, the recording secretary, noted that one evening Mr Chase gave a 'helpful and beautiful talk' at the Ackerknecht home.[423]

Isabella Brittingham introduced Ella Quant to the Bahá'ís on Sunday afternoon, 15 March 1903, at a meeting at Sophia and Fred Ackerknect's home. Ella had been studying with Isabella for some weeks, and it is possible that she became a member of the community in March or shortly afterwards. At the request of the House of Spirituality in Chicago, Johnstown held its first Naw-Rúz commemoration that same month at its regular weekly meeting on the 25th. On this occasion one of the friends read 'Abdu'l-Bahá's eulogy of Thomas Breakwell, the first English believer, who had recently died in Paris. Isabella did not attend this event, as she had left Johnstown four days earlier for Chicago on the first leg of an extended teaching trip.

In the autumn of 1903 Ella received her first Tablet from 'Abdu'l-Bahá. Dated 1 August, it was delivered to her by Isabella Brittingham and read, in part:

> He is God. I ask God to make thee firm in His religion, to confirm thee through the Breath of the Holy Spirit, so that thou mayest speak forth the teachings of God and guide the people into the Kingdom . . . Verily, the bounty of God upon thee is great! If thou remaineth firm in the path of the love of God, thou shalt behold the doors of success and progress open before thy face from all sides . . . [424]

The Johnstown community continued to grow after Ella joined it and the teaching work was extended. For example, in its report of 21 February 1904 the Assembly notes that 'Mrs May Simpson, who has recently accepted the Faith, met with us for the first time and we were delighted to have her with us'.[425] In March Ella presented Myron Phelps's book *The Life and Teachings of Abbas Effendi* to the Johnstown library, receiving a note of grateful acknowledgement from the librarian, Mary France.[426]

Ella was an active member of the Bahá'í community. In the autumn of 1904 she took over the role of secretary for the period 3 October to 4 December, reporting on various meetings held in Johnstown and keeping the minutes. She notes, for example, that at the meeting of 9 October 'the first pages of the Book of Assurance . . . from the pen of the Blessed Perfection, Bahá'u'lláh, were read; successive passages of the Book will be read at the spiritual gatherings on Sundays until the Book is completed.'[427] Of the meeting on 16 October she wrote:

> Our hearts were cheered by having three visitors. After the regular meeting a talk on the truth (setting forth the need of a Manifestation in this day and the signs of the end as now being fulfilled) was given for the benefit of the visitors who seemed interested. We now sow the seed. – The increase is from our God.[428]

As Ella walked towards the Ackerknecht home on Thursday evening, 27 October, for the regular mid-week meeting of the Bahá'í community, she had a vision of the future:

> After passing a church in which a service was being held, beautiful inspiring thoughts came to my mind. I seemed to see the names of the few Bahá'ís, the faithful ones, exalted as Bahá'u'lláh has said they will be above all who have gone before. I thought of the Master's words to the Johnstown Assembly, and it seemed that I could see the day in which the believers had filled the town, and I could see the lofty edifices (with spiral fingers ever pointing upward) built by the Bahá'ís of Johnstown and I heard a song . . . the Might, the Power, the Glory of which we as yet do not comprehend – Alláh-u-Abhá![429]

At the meeting that evening the friends studied passages from Isabella Brittingham's booklet *The Revelation of Bahá-Ulláh*, perhaps this one among them:

When the soul hungers for the knowledge of its God, and it drinks from the unadulterated 'Cup of Immortality', that crystal draught, in its action upon that soul, resembles a drop of elixir upon a piece of copper, which cleansing from all impurity, man arises from the animal station (the station of sensation which is our Satan) and attains the station of intellect; then dies to that station and arises in the station of spirit. It has been said that 'the last degree of reason is the first degree of love'.[430]

Active though she was in the community, Ella was not able to host meetings in her own home. On 17 November 1904 Mrs Emily Gustian offered her home to Ella so that she might enjoy the privilege of leading the meeting.[431]

The Brittinghams were perhaps the most active teachers in Johnstown and a decline in the rate of growth of the Bahá'í community in the town coincided with their move to northern New Jersey in 1904.[432] However, Isabella Brittingham did not sever her links with Johnstown completely. She visited the town early in 1906 to explain to the Bahá'ís there the nature of the Nineteen Day Feast and to inaugurate it as a 'formal community event'.[433]

In November 1907 the Chicago House of Spirituality held a convention of delegates to consider the building of the first Bahá'í House of Worship in America. Although the Johnstown Bahá'ís were unable to attend, they did respond to a circular letter sent by the Chicago Bahá'ís by offering their support to the project. Ella wrote, 'We do not feel that it is a Temple for Chicago alone, but for *every* soul who breathes His Name, indeed for all peoples to come.'[434] When the Johnstown Bahá'ís received another circular letter seeking support for the Temple, they responded by establishing a 'local Temple branch' on 9 April 1908, with Margaret La Grange as the secretary and Ella as treasurer.[435] In 1910 Ella went to the second annual convention of the Bahá'í Temple Unity, held in the Corinthian Hall, Chicago, on 25 and 26 April, as a delegate from Johnstown and six other Bahá'í groups in central New York state – Hudson, Utica, Clinton,

Cortland, Oswego and Buffalo. She gave a short address at the Bahá'í Festival Service on the morning before the convention.[436]

Ella received a second Tablet from 'Abdu'l-Bahá in November 1909. He praised Ella, gave her advice and encouraged her to teach the Cause and 'exhorted her to give thanks to her teacher, Mrs Brittingham'.[437]

Ella continued to report the events of the Johnstown Bahá'ís in the Bahá'í News. In the 5 June 1910 edition, for example, she wrote:

> The Bahá'í Assembly of Johnstown, New York, holds regular meetings at the home of Mrs Emily Gustian. The Nineteen Day feast or Supper of the Lord is also regularly observed . . . Hudson, Mica, Cortland, Pavilion and Oswego, N. Y., each has a believer – Oswego two to uphold the standard of the Cause . . . If travelling Bahá'ís can visit any of these above named places much good will be done in strengthening these isolated ones . . . May the blessing and love in His Name be upon every soul. Praise God, the Day of Unity is dawning wherein the Mashriqu'l-Adhkár is to be built.[438]

In March 1911 'Abdu'l-Bahá sent a Tablet to 23 named Bahá'ís, including Ella, in New York state:

> O ye who are attracted to the Beauty of Abhá!
>
> Your letter was received. It indicated that a new union and harmony is created among those souls. This glad tidings produced a great happiness and a new hope was seized that perchance the friends of New York, God willing, may become united and harmonized with the heavenly power. Today the most beloved and acceptable deed before His Highness, Bahá'u'lláh, is the union of the friends and the concord of men, and the most unacceptable is difference and inharmony.
>
> Praised be to God that ye have become assisted with this Most Great Bounty, that is, unity and harmony, and become the cause of the happiness of 'Abdu'l-Bahá . . .[439]

A year later, 'Abdu'l-Bahá was in New York and Ella found

herself in the company of many other Bahá'ís on the pier as
His ship docked. She and Margaret La Grange had travelled
to New York City the day before to await His arrival.
On the afternoon of 11 April 1912 Ella and Margaret
went to see 'Abdu'l-Bahá:

> When we arrived at the home of Mr and Mrs Kinney, the
> rooms were crowded with the friends and 'Abdu'l-Bahá was
> mingling freely among them radiating the spiritual happi-
> ness He said He felt in meeting the 'friends of God'.[440]

'Abdu'l-Bahá addressed the friends, saying, 'I am greatly
pleased with New York' and expressing the hope that as New
York had made such good material progress, 'it may also
advance spiritually in the kingdom and covenant of God'.[441]
Ella recalls:

> At the end of this address 'Abdu'l-Bahá greeted each one
> personally, clasping the hand and repeating the word,
> 'Marhabá! Marhabá!' (Welcome! Welcome!) with such
> fervour that I could not fail to grasp His meaning, though
> unfamiliar with the word.[442]

Ella was in the presence of 'Abdu'l-Bahá several times during
her five-day stay in New York. She longed for a private
interview with Him, such as other Bahá'ís had been granted:

> The interpreter said the Master was very busy, but, nothing
> daunted, Margaret explained to him that we were from out
> of town and longed for an interview before leaving New
> York. So the matter was finally arranged and on Sunday
> morning at nine we found ourselves being ushered into the
> presence of 'Abdu'l-Bahá, and in English He was addressing
> us with the words, Sit down, sit down, as He courteously
> showed us to seats . . . His next words awakened us to our
> immediate environment. He said He was happy to have
> such souls as we were: Rest thou assured, rest thou assured,
> and, we had come some distance to meet Him and had
> passed through difficulties, but He had come farther to
> meet us.

Such words we were not prepared to hear; knowing that we were humble people and feeling we had but small capacity to serve the Faith of Bahá'u'lláh, we could not understand such words applying to ourselves.

. . . when I asked the interpreter to tell Him I wished to serve Him always, He called me His daughter. He then said, Your face is radiant.[443]

Later that day, 14 April, Palm Sunday, Ella and Margaret attended the now famous service at the Church of the Ascension on Fifth Avenue and Tenth Street where 'Abdu'l-Bahá gave His first public address in America. Ella recalls the 'unforgettable picture – 'Abdu'l-Bahá standing among the lilies.'[444]

Ella remembers her other audiences with the Master:

Our second meeting with 'Abdu'l-Bahá was on April 12, in the studio of Miss Phillips. In connection with this meeting, I must go into a little detail that will show all too clearly my immaturity in the ethics of the Kingdom. As Margaret and I entered the spacious room we observed our beloved 'Abdu'l-Bahá sitting on a couch, a young Persian on either side of Him. Shortly one of the devoted friends of the Master entered and one of the Persians sitting beside 'Abdu'l-Bahá arose and offered his seat to the lady, which she accepted. I was disturbed and said to myself, 'Oh! Who is worthy to sit beside 'Abdu'l-Bahá?' The question bothered me all evening, but was relegated to the background of my mind save at such times as I found myself alone with my thoughts . . .

Later, in leaving, as 'Abdu'l-Bahá took my hand, I was conscious of His eyes partially raised to mine. Did He see there the unanswered question of the early evening: Who is worthy to sit beside 'Abdu'l-Bahá?

On the following Monday, the last day we were privileged to be in His holy presence, He deigned to answer my question. After greeting us He seated Margaret on a chair near Him at just the right angle, she told me later, where she might look into His eyes; thus fulfilling a desire of hers. Then, He seated *me on the couch beside Him* and turned on me (the questioner) the smile of His divine love, which penetrated my physical and spiritual consciousness. Thus did He teach us, the friends, everywhere, not by rebuke, but with touching example, that the Sun of God's bounty shines upon all and only the veils of self hide us from an ever-increasing realization of its effulgence.[445]

Ella had been in poor health for some time and was finding it difficult to carry out her household responsibilities. 'I was brought up in the old-fashioned way that assumed the house could not be clean unless one had a backache.' At this last meeting with 'Abdu'l-Bahá, He enquired about her health and told her 'decrease physical labour, work not beyond the extent of your strength, turn toward the Kingdom of God; strength is from God; divine confirmation shall descend; you shall attain to physical health; rest assured of the favour of God'. Ella said of this advice, 'More than once through the years these words of the Master have kept not only my physical balance, but the mental and spiritual as well.'[446]

Just before Ella had left home for New York she had dreamed that she and another Bahá'í were standing before a vast expanse of water. In the years since becoming a Bahá'í Ella had had several such dreams from which she had attempted to derive some spiritual meaning. Now, at this farewell interview, 'Abdu'l-Bahá interpreted Ella's dream. He said that 'in the dream the sea is the Kingdom, and that is the Cause of God. That I with that other Bahá'í shall attain to the shore of that Sea, and shall behold its expanse.'[447]

Ella and Margaret returned home to Johnstown, never again to attain the presence of 'Abdu'l-Bahá.

Ella continued to serve the Faith conscientiously. In 1919 she was a delegate to the eleventh annual convention of the Bahá'í Temple Unity, named by 'Abdu'l-Bahá the 'Convention of the Covenant', which together with the Bahá'í Congress took place at the Hotel McAlpin in New York City in April. She gave a 'spiritual and uplifting' report at the second session of the convention.[448]

In July 1919 Ella received a third Tablet from 'Abdu'l-

Bahá, translated by 'Shoghi Rabbani, Bahjeh, Acca, Palestine, July 20, 1919':

> To the maid-servant of God, Ella Quant, New York City, N.Y. – Upon her be Baha'o'llah El-Abha!
>
> He is God!
>
> O thou daughter of the Kingdom!
> Thy letter was received. It was indicative of thy attendance at the convention where thou hast witnessed the lights of the divine teachings resplendent and hast seen the souls vivified by the spirit of everlasting life. As thou wert endowed with the power of insight, thou hast in this manner discovered Truth. Whoever is firm in the Covenant and the Testament is today endowed with a seeing eye, and a responsive ear and daily advances in the divine realm until he becomes a heavenly angel . . . [449]

The Tablet no doubt inspired Ella even further in her devotion to the Cause of Bahá'u'lláh.

At their regular monthly meeting of 30 December 1919, the Bahá'ís of Johnstown, acting on Ella's suggestion, decided to advertise, at their own expense, the basic principles of the Faith in the local newspapers. George Williams, of nearby Gloversville, read these advertisements and began to study the teachings of the Faith more fully. Some months later, through the efforts of Margaret La Grange, he became a Bahá'í.[450]

At some point Ella moved from Johnstown to Schenectady, New York. In June of 1940 she was the only believer there. The Regional Teaching Committee of Upper New York State reported in the *Bahá'í News* that Ella had arranged to have the model of the first Mashriqu'l-Adhkár exhibited in the local museum for several weeks and for Allen McDaniel to speak there about the importance of the building. The next year a report in the *Bahá'í News* stated that in Schenectady Ella had 'given out Braille literature for the blind, called on minority groups, addressed a meeting in a Negro church, whose minister suggested that a class be formed to study the Bahá'í teachings, and she has kept in touch with this congregation'.[451] By 1946 Schenectady had a Bahá'í group that 'maintains a reading room and gives monthly public meetings'.[452]

Ella was a Braillist and a member of the Bahá'í Committee on Braille Transcription for many years, serving some of that time as its chairman. The purpose of the committee was 'to provide Bahá'í literature in Braille for the blind; to place Bahá'í Braille literature in libraries and other institutions; to encourage the formation of groups of Bahá'í workers; to increase the supply of Braille transcription'.[453]

Ella made Braille transcriptions of many Bahá'í works: *Divine Philosophy*, 'Words of Wisdom', *Prayers* and *Bahá'í Teachings on Economics*, among others.[454] In 1937 the then chairman Mrs Samuel Redman reported that the committee's outstanding achievement of the year was the transcription into Braille of the Esperanto translation of *The Bahá'í Revelation* (*La Bahaa Revelacia*) by Ella Quant. Pleased that there was an increasing demand for Braille Bahá'í literature, Shoghi Effendi wrote to the committee: 'Persevere, nay redouble your efforts. I am planning to establish in the Mansion of Bahjí a special section wholly and exclusively devoted to Bahá'í literature in Braille.'[455]

In the *Bahá'í News* of April 1938 Mrs Redman listed 14 books and pamphlets transcribed into Braille by Ella, calling her work 'an achievement of great merit'.[456] In 1941, when Ella was chairman, she pointed out the importance of Braille literature:

> Shoghi Effendi always stressed the importance of the Braille work, and a believer who has international contacts told me recently that many taking part in the great tragedy of war are becoming blind and deaf from the shattering of nerves. What a bounty it is to be able to braille the Holy Writings for such souls, that their spiritual sight and hearing may be quickened.[457]

The next year Ella was able to report a remarkable achievement: Mrs Bahiyyih Valentine of New York City had, at the age of 86, completed the Braille course and had received a certificate as a Certified Braille Transcriber from the National Red Cross.[458] Mrs Valentine lived to be New York's oldest resident and remained an active Bahá'í until her death at the age of 99. In her annual report for 1942-3, Ella noted that Mrs Valentine was the only one to make a contribution that year to the reserve library, having transcribed 'The Golden Age of the Cause'.[459]

By 1944 the Committee of Braille Transcription had become the 'Bahá'í Service for the Blind'. Ella described its 'two-fold objective':

> to enlarge the reserve library, thereby increasing its capacity to serve; also to establish a system of 'Talking Books' for the blind who do not read Braille; that in the Centennial Year of the Glorious Manifestation of Bahá'u'lláh he who is physically sightless may be able to say in spirit – 'Although once I was blind, but now I see'.[460]

Ella occasionally wrote for *World Order* magazine. In 1937 she published 'I Will Come Again':

> I have met many people whose love for Jesus and His word was apparently sincere; yet these same people when questioned concerning the Promise 'I will come again' spoken by Jesus to His disciples, answer as though all is like a fast-fading star in their consciousness . . . After giving much thought and study to the subject, I have reached the following conclusion: 'The intellect is unable to accept literal interpretations of portions of Bible prophecy, bearing on the subject of the "Second Coming"; consequently the Christian today has lost that most vital part of his religion – faith in the Promise of Jesus concerning His return.'
>
> . . . There can be no proselytizing in true religion. One does not give up one truth for another truth, but as the soul develops spiritually, the inner eye becomes keener and more accustomed to the glorious panorama that spreads before it.[461]

In 1943 Ella sent the editors of *World Order* an essay entitled 'The City of God', enclosing a note vividly describing her feelings in the spring of 1903 when Mrs Brittingham told her of the Bahá'í Faith:

> The grass was greener, the song birds sweeter, all nature was happy with me, and, in my own experience I could verify all that the poets had ever written about love – for a I knew that my Beloved had come. The new name and the new garment accentuated the sweetness of His Presence.[462]

Referring to Shoghi Effendi's position as the Guardian of the Cause of God, she wrote:

> It is a miracle for each soul . . . Shoghi Effendi has so loved me, cheered and encouraged me, insignificant as I am, that I lack words to express it all. Whatever the Master planted in me, Shoghi Effendi has watered and tended with divine love.[463]

On the development of the Faith she added this note: 'There was a time when it seemed that I knew and corresponded with every believer, but how the Cause has grown.'[464]

Ella was housebound for some time during the winter of 1942-3. She used her time to write another article for *Bahá'í World*: 'This winter being housed for some weeks I have had such a strong urge to write 'The Bahá'í Feast' that now I am sending it to you.'[465]

> What a difference between so-called 'good times' and the Bahá'í Feasts of joy! Here the laughter wells up from the heart; here the smile is a happy one – for Bahá'ís know that there is a God, for He has again in His love manifested Himself to mankind. Bahá'ís know the Sun is shining, in spite of the dark clouds that would hide its radiance. Bahá'ís know that the springtime has again come, although the chill winds of the soul's winter are still felt.[466]

When Ella was in her eighties, in 1963, she went on her 'first international teaching trip', visiting small Bahá'í communities in western Ontario. On her return she reported to the Canadian National Teaching Committee:

I feel I must assure you, as I have been assured, of the many wonderfully dedicated Bahá'ís it has been my privilege to meet. I am not a trained speaker, neither do I think of myself as a Bahá'í teacher, the distinguishing feature of my life being the five days spent 'In the Presence of 'Abdu'l-Bahá' in New York City . . .

I believe the birth of the first Universal House of Justice (1963) has propelled the Bahá'í world into a new era, in which we can no longer fail to recognize the great responsibility placed upon the Local Spiritual Assemblies. We must indeed, I feel, work towards a unity of understanding effort . . . and working more and more fully towards a oneness of decision, becoming truly as a strong pillar supporting this marvellous institution of the Faith of Bahá'u'lláh, the Universal House of Justice . . .[467]

Ella died in November 1971 and was buried on 15 November. A year later 16 Bahá'ís gathered to place over her grave a rose-tinted granite headstone:

Dearly Loved Bahá'í
Ella C. Quant

Bibliography

'Abdu'l-Bahá, *The Promulgation of Universal Peace.* Wilmette, Ill.: Bahá'í Publishing Trust, 2nd edn. 1982.
— *The Tablets of the Divine Plan.* Wilmette, Ill.: Bahá'í Publishing Trust, rev. edn. 1977.
— *The Will and Testament of 'Abdu'l-Bahá.* Wilmette, Ill.: Bahá'í Publishing Trust, 1971.
Annual Report of the National Spiritual Assembly of the Bahá'ís of the United States and Canada 1938-1939.
Annual Report of the National Spiritual Assembly of the Bahá'ís of the United States and Canada 1940-1941.
Bahá'í International News Service, 6 June 1981.
The Bahá'í Magazine, vol. 16, no. 9.
Bahá'í News: January 1901, 17 May 1910, 5 June 1910, 13 July 1910, July 1930, July 1931, September 1931, December 1931, February 1931, June 1935, April 1937, April 1938, November 1938, December 1938, May 1939, March 1941, November 1941, February 1942, July 1942, January 1944, September 1944, March 1949, April 1949, June 1953, February 1962, July 1962, October 1973; August 1981; vol. 1, no. 1; vol. 1. no. 4; vol. 1, no. 5; vol. 1, no. 10; vol. 1, no. 13; vol. 2, no. 4.
Bahá'í News Annual Reports 1942-3.
Bahá'í News Annual Report 1945-6.
Bahá'í News Letter: January 1925, January 1930.
Bahá'í World, The. vol. 4, Wilmette, Ill.: Bahá'í Publishing Trust, 1933, rpt. 1980; vol. 5, New York City: Bahá'í Publishing Committee, 1936; vol. 7, Wilmette, Ill.: Bahá'í Publishing Trust, 1939, rpt. 1980; vol. 8, Wilmette, Ill.: Bahá'í Publishing Committee, 1942; vol. 9, Wilmette, Ill.: Bahá'í Publishing Committee, 1945; vol. 10, Wilmette, Ill.: Bahá'í Publishing Trust, 1949, rpt. 1981; vol. 11, Wilmette, Ill.: Bahá'í Publishing Committee, 1952; vol. 12, Wilmette, Ill.: Bahá'í Publishing Trust, 1956, rpt. 1981; vol. 13, Haifa, Israel: The Universal House of Justice, 1970; vol. 15, Haifa: Bahá'í World Centre, 1976.

Bahá'u'lláh. *Gleanings from the Writings of Bahá'u'lláh*. Wilmette, Ill.: Bahá'í Publishing Trust, 1983.

— *Tablets of Bahá'u'lláh revealed after the Kitáb-i-Aqdas*. Haifa: Bahá'í World Centre, 1978.

Balyuzi, H. M. *'Abdu'l-Bahá*. Oxford: George Ronald, 1971.

Blomfield, Lady. *The Chosen Highway*. London: Bahá'í Publishing Trust, 1940.

Brittingham, Isabella D. *The Revelation of Bahä-Ulläh in a Sequence of Four Lessons*. Chicago: Bahai Publishing Society, 1902.

Brown, Ramona Allen. *Memories of 'Abdu'l-Bahá*.Wilmette, Ill.: Bahá'í Publishing Trust, 1980.

Esslemont, John E. *Bahá'u'lláh and the New Era*. London: Bahá'í Publishing Trust, 1974.

Faizi, Abu'l-Qásim. *A Flame of Fire*. New Delhi: Bahá'í Publishing Trust, 1969.

— *Milly, A Tribute to the Hand of the Cause of God Amelia E. Collins*. Oxford: George Ronald, 1977.

Giachery, Ugo. *Shoghi Effendi, Recollections*. Oxford: George Ronald, 1973.

Honnold, Annamarie. 'Notes on My Mother, Anna Kunz', February 1985.

— *Vignettes from the Life of 'Abdu'l-Bahá*. Oxford: George Ronald, 1982.

Kunz-Ruhe, Margaret. 'Biography of Anna Kunz', no date.

Momen, Moojan. *Dr John Ebenezer Esslemont M.B., Ch.B., SBEA, Hand of the Cause of God*. London: Bahá'í Publishing Trust, 1975.

Quant, Ella. 'I Will Come Again'. *World Order*, August 1937.

— 'Some Notes on the History of the Bahá'í Faith in Johnstown', manuscript.

Rabbaní, Rúḥíyyih. *The Priceless Pearl*. London: Bahá'í Publishing Trust, 1969.

Sala, Rosemary. 'Notes about Mrs Collins', manuscript.

Shoghi Effendi. *Bahá'í Administration*. Wilmette, Ill.: Bahá'í Publishing Trust, 1974.

— *Citadel of Faith: Messages to America 1947-1957*. Wilmette, Ill.: Bahá'í Publishing Trust, 1965.

— *Dawn of a New Day: Messages to India 1923-1957*. New Delhi: Bahá'í Publishing Trust, 1970.

— *God Passes By*. Wilmette, Ill.: Bahá'í Publishing Trust, rev. edn. 1974.

— *Messages to America: Selected Letters and Cablegrams Addressed to the Bahá'ís of North America, 1932-1946.* Wilmette, Ill.: Bahá'í Publishing Committee, 1947.

— *Messages to the Bahá'í World 1950-1957.* Wilmette, Ill.: Bahá'í Publishing Trust, 1958.

— *The Unfolding Destiny of the British Bahá'í Community.* London: Bahá'í Publishing Trust, 1981.

Star of the West, vol. 2, no 5; vol. 2, no. 16; vol. 3, no. 4; vol. 3, no. 7; vol. 3, no. 11; vol. 4, no. 8; vol. 4, no. 17; vol. 5, no. 4; vol. 7, no. 7; vol. 8, no. 9; vol. 8, no. 10; vol. 8, no. 13; vol. 8, no. 14; vol. 8, no. 19; vol. 9, no. 4; vol. 9, no. 5; vol. 9, no. 17; vol. 10, no. 3; vol. 10, no. 4; vol. 10, no. 13; vol. 10, no. 18; vol. 11, no. 11; vol. 12, no. 10; vol. 13, no. 1; vol. 13, no. 1; vol. 13, no. 6; vol. 13,no. 8; vol. 14, no. 3;

Stebbins, Joel. 'Jakob Kunz, 1874-1938'. *Popular Astronomy,* vol. 17, no. 3 (March 1939).

Stockman, Robert *Bahá'í Faith in America,* vol. 2. Oxford: George Ronald, 1995.

World Order, March 1943, September 1943, June 1945, March 1949.

References

1. De Mille, 'Emogene Hoagg', *Bahá'í News*, October 1973, p. 6.
2. Cooper, 'Henrietta Emogene Martin Hoagg', *Bahá'í World*, vol. 10, p. 520.
3. De Mille, 'Emogene Hoagg', *Bahá'í News*, October 1973, p. 6.
4. ibid.
5. ibid. p. 7.
6. Cooper, 'Henrietta Emogene Martin Hoagg', *Bahá'í World*, vol. 10, p. 520.
7. De Mille, 'Emogene Hoagg', *Bahá'í News*, October 1973, p. 7.
8. ibid.
9. ibid.
10. Cooper, 'Henrietta Emogene Martin Hoagg', *Bahá'í World*, vol. 10, p. 520.
11. ibid. pp. 520-1.
12. De Mille, 'Emogene Hoagg', *Bahá'í News*, October 1973, p. 6.
13. 'Abdu'l-Bahá, cited in Cooper, 'Henrietta Emogene Martin Hoagg', *Bahá'í World*, vol. 10, p. 525.
14. De Mille, 'Emogene Hoagg', *Bahá'í News*, October 1973, p. 8.
15. Shoghi Effendi, *God Passes By*, pp. 261-2.
16. De Mille, 'Emogene Hoagg', *Bahá'í News*, October 1973, p. 8.
17. Hannen, 'With Abdul-Baha in Dublin, New Hampshire', *Star of the West*, vol. 3, no. 11, pp. 3-4.
18. De Mille, 'Emogene Hoagg', *Bahá'í News*, October 1973, p. 8.
19. Balyuzi, *'Abdu'l-Bahá*, p. 400.
20. De Mille, 'Emogene Hoagg', *Bahá'í News*, October 1973, p. 8.
21. ibid.
22. Emogene Hoagg, letter to Charles Mason Remey, 27 December 1913, in *Star of the West*, vol. 4, no. 17, pp. 288-90.

23. Words of Munírih <u>Kh</u>ánum, quoted by Emogene Hoagg in a letter dated 1914, in *Star of the West*, vol. 8, no. 13, p. 158.
24. Balyuzi, *'Abdu'l-Bahá*, pp. 230, 407.
25. 'Bahai Temple Unity Convention', *Star of the West*, vol. 8, no. 10, p. 133.
26. *Star of the West*, vol. 8, no. 14, pp. 200-1.
27. 'Abdu'l-Bahá, *Tablets of the Divine Plan*, p. 15.
28. Foreword to 'Abdu'l-Bahá, *Tablets of the Divine Plan*, pp. x-xi.
29. *Star of the West*, vol. 10, no. 4, pp. 54-63.
30. 'Abdu'l-Bahá, *Tablets of the Divine Plan*, p. 31.
31. ibid. p. 95.
32. Cooper, 'Henrietta Emogene Martin Hoagg', *Bahá'í World*, vol. 10, p. 122.
33. Shoghi Effendi, *Citadel of Faith*, p. 165.
34. 'Marion Jack', *Bahá'í World*, vol. 12, pp. 674-7.
35. Hudson and Kolstoe, 'Alaska: Planting the Seeds of Victory', *Bahá'í News*, August 1981, pp. 6-9.
36. De Mille, 'Emogene Hoagg', *Bahá'í News*, October 1973, p. 9.
37. Hudson and Kolstoe, 'Alaska: Planting the Seeds of Victory', *Bahá'í News*, August 1981, p. 7.
38. De Mille, 'Emogene Hoagg', *Bahá'í News*, October 1973, p. 9.
39. Hudson and Kolstoe, 'Alaska: Planting the Seeds of Victory', *Bahá'í News*, August 1981, pp. 7-8.
40. ibid. p. 8.
41. Cooper, 'Henrietta Emogene Martin Hoagg', *Bahá'í World*, vol. 10, p. 522.
42. ibid.
43. ibid.
44. ibid. pp. 122-3.
45. ibid. p. 523.
46. Hudson and Kolstoe, 'Alaska: Planting the Seeds of Victory', *Bahá'í News*, August 1981, p. 8.
47. *Star of the West*, vol. 11, no. 11, p. 196.
48. Coy, 'A Week in Abdul-Baha's Home', *Star of the West*, vol. 12, no. 10, p. 165. This article was carried over across several issues.
49. ibid. vol. 12, no. 13, pp. 212-13.

50. De Mille, 'Emogene Hoagg', *Bahá'í News*, October 1973, p. 9.
51. ibid. pp. 9-10.
52. ibid.
53. 'Abdu'l-Bahá, in *Star of the West*, vol. 13, no. 1, p. 19.
54. De Mille, 'Emogene Hoagg', *Bahá'í News*, October 1973, p. 10.
55. ibid.
56. ibid.
57. Letter from Emogene Hoagg to Corinne True, 24 January 1922, in *Star of the West*, vol. 13, no. 1, p. 26.
58. Shoghi Effendi, *God Passes By*, p. 380.
59. Hoagg, 'Short History of the International Bahá'í Bureau', *Bahá'í World*, vol. 4, p. 257.
60. Warde, 'Julia Culver', *Bahá'í World*, vol. 11, p. 508.
61. *Bahá'í News*, April 1938, p. 9.
62. ibid. p. 22.
63. *Bahá'í News*, November 1938, p. 6.
64. ibid. p. 7.
65. *Bahá'í News*, December 1938, p. 4.
66. Annual Report of the National Spiritual Assembly of the Bahá'ís of the United States and Canada 1938-1939, p. 39.
67. Hoagg, 'Conditions of Existence: Servitude, Prophethood, Deity', p. iii.
68. *Bahá'í News*, May 1939, p. 7.
69. Bahá'u'lláh, *Gleanings*, p. 150.
70. Ginés, 'The Story of the Bahá'í Faith in Cuba', *Bahá'í World*, vol. 9, p. 916.
71. Annual Report of the National Spiritual Assembly of the Bahá'ís of the United States and Canada 1940-1941, p. 12.
72. Ginés, 'The Story of the Bahá'í Faith in Cuba', *Bahá'í World*, vol. 9, p. 916; *Bahá'í News*, May 1941, p. 6.
73. Gail, 'The Historic Thirty-Sixth Convention', *Bahá'í News*, September 1944, p. 14.
74. De Mille, 'Emogene Hoagg', *Bahá'í News*, October 1973, p. 11.
75. 'Hoagg, 'The Tablets of 'Abdu'l-Bahá', *World Order*, June 1945, p. 87.
76. Josephine Pinson, quoted in De Mille, 'Emogene Hoagg', *Bahá'í News*, October 1973, p. 11.
77. Shoghi Effendi, quoted in ibid.

78. Cooper, 'Henrietta Emogene Martin Hoagg', *Bahá'í World*, vol. 10, p. 524.
79. The devoted Bahá'í Claudia Kelly has often spoken to me about her beloved grandmother Claudia Stuart Coles with much interest and affection. She wrote me several letters in 1983, providing more information about Mrs Coles, saying, 'I am thrilled that you plan to research my grandmother's life. I shall assist you all that I can.' Letter from Claudia Kelly to author, 15 April 1983.
80. Undated letter from Claudia Kelly to author, received in March 1983.
81. Letter from Claudia Kelly to author, 25 August 1983.
82. ibid.
83. ibid.
84. Tablet revealed by 'Abdu'l-Bahá for Claudia Stuart Coles, translated by M. A. Esphahani, 9 December 1906 at 2:00 p.m. at Washington DC.
85. Tablet revealed by 'Abdu'l-Bahá for an unnamed believer, translated 16 February 1907 by M. A. Esphahani.
86. Tablet revealed by 'Abdu'l-Bahá for Claudia Stuart Coles, 21 June 1907, translated by M.A. Esphahani 1 August 1907.
87. *Bahai News*, vol. 1, no. 1, p. 4.
88. *Bahai News*, vol. 1, no 4, pp. 18, 20.
89. 'Abdu'l-Bahá, quoted in *Bahai News*, vol. 1, no. 5, p. 3.
90. *Bahai News*, vol. 1, no. 10, p. 5.
91. *Bahai News*, vol. 1, no. 13, pp. 6-7.
92. 'Abdu'l-Bahá, cited in *Bahai News*, vol. 2, no. 4, pp. 6-7.
93. ibid. p. 4.
94. ibid. p. 14.
95. ibid. p. 5.
96. Blomfield, *Chosen Highway*, p. 151.
97. Undated letter from Claudia Kelly to the author, received March 1983.
98. Tablet of 'Abdu'l-Bahá to Claudia Coles, *Star of the West*, vol. 2, no. 16, p. 7.
99. Claudia Coles, quoted in ibid.
100. *Star of the West*, vol. 3, no. 4, p. 4.
101. ibid. p. 32.
102. 'Abdu'l-Bahá, *Promulgation*, pp. 65-6.
103. *Star of the West*, vol. 3, no. 4, p. 5.

104. ibid. p. 6.
105. *Star of the West*, vol. 4, no. 8, p. 146.
106. ibid. p. 134.
107. Mariam Haney, In memorium of Claudia Coles, *Bahá'í News*, no. 53, July 1931, p. 7.
108. ibid.
109. *Star of the West*, vol. 5, no. 4, p. 55.
110. *Star of the West*, vol. 7, no. 7, p. 65.
111. *Star of the West*, vol. 8, no. 9, p. 115.
112. 'Centennial Celebration of the Birth of Baha'o'llah', *Star of the West*, vol. 8, no. 14, p. 191.
113. ibid. p. 199.
114. *Star of the West*, vol. 9, no. 4, p. 49.
115. *Star of the West*, vol. 9, mo. 5, p. 71.
116. 'Extracts from the Diary of Major Wellesly Tudor-Pole', *Star of the West*, vol. 9, no. 17, pp. 187, 192.
117. *Star of the West*, vol. 10, no. 3, p. 43.
118. *Star of the West*, vol. 10, no. 4, p. 63.
119. Momen, *Esslemont*, pp. 19, 21, 22, 43, 28.
120. Esslemont, *Bahá'u'lláh and the New Era*, p. x.
121. Undated letter from Claudia Kelly to the author, received March 1983.
122. Rabbani, *Priceless Pearl*, p. 102.
123. Shoghi Effendi, *Bahá'í Administration*, p. 97.
124. Tablet of 'Abdu'l-Bahá revealed for Claudia Stuart Coles, translated by Mírzá Ahmad Sohrab Moyist in Washington DC, 1910.
125. Helen F. Grand, 'How I became a Bahá'í', *The Bahá'í Magazine*, pp. 363-4.
126. Letter from Richard St Barbe Baker to Mabel Garis, 18 February 1981.
127. Letter from Claudia Kelly to the author, 25 August 1983.
128. Richard St Barbe Baker, 'The Men of the Trees', *Bahá'í World*, vol. 5, p. 552.
129. Letter from Richard St Barbe Baker to Martha Root, 7 February 1935.
130. Claudia Stuart Coles, 'To Make Holy', *The Bahá'í Magazine*, vol. 16, no. 9, pp. 642-3.
131. Letter of Claudia Coles to Julia Culver, 13 June 1926.
132. 'New Letter From Bahá'ís of the British Isles', *Bahá'í News Letter*, January 1930, p. 7.

133. 'News letter from Bahá'ís of the British Isles', *Bahá'í News*, July 1930, p. 8.
134. Shoghi Effendi, *Unfolding Destiny*, p. 88.
135. 'News Letter from Bahá'ís of British Isles', *Bahá'í News*, July 1930, p. 8.
136. Shoghi Effendi, *Citadel of Faith*, p. 168.
137. 'Bahá'í Activities in Other Lands – Great Britain', *Bahá'í News*, September 1931, p. 6.
138. Shoghi Effendi, in *Bahá'í News*, July 1931, p. 7.
139. Letter from Richard St Barbe Baker to Evelyn Aldridge, 28 August 1931, in the possession of Claudia Kelly.
140. Letter from Claudia Kelly to the author, 25 August 1983.
141. Margaret Kunz-Ruhe, 'Biography of Anna Kunz', p. 1.
142. Annamarie Honnold, 'Notes on My Mother, Anna Kunz', February 1985, p. 5.
143. ibid. p. 1.
144. ibid. p. 4.
145. ibid. pp. 1, 4.
146. ibid. p. 4.
147. Joel Stebbins, 'Jakob Kunz, 1874-1938, *Popular Astronomy*, vol. 17, no. 3 (March 1939), p. 1.
148. Annamarie Honnold, 'Notes on My Mother, Anna Kunz', p. 2.
149. Stebbins, 'Jakob Kunz, 1874-1938', *Popular Astronomy*, vol. 17, no. 3 (March 1939), p. 1.
150. Annamarie Honnold, 'Notes on My Mother, Anna Kunz', p. 2.
151. Joel Stebbins, 'Jakob Kunz 1874-1938', *Popular Astronomy*, vol. 17, no. 3 (March 1939), p. 1.
152. ibid.
153. Annamarie Honnold, 'Notes on My Mother, Anna Kunz'.
154. Margaret Kunz-Ruhe, 'Biography of Anna Kunz'.
155. Cited in a letter from Chris Ruhe-Schoen to the author, 7 March 1985.
156. ibid.
157. Shoghi Effendi, *God Passes By*, pp. 307-8, 375.
158. Anna Kunz, 'Some Questions about Science and Religion', *Star of the West*, vol. 13, no. 6, pp. 139-40.
159. ibid. p. 140.
160. ibid. p. 140.
161. ibid. p. 142.

162. ibid. p. 143.
163. ibid.
164. ibid.
165. 'Abdu'l-Bahá, translated by Azizullah Khan S. Bahadur at Tiberias, cited in Margaret Kunz-Ruhe, 'Biography of Anna Kunz', p. 8.
166. ibid. p. 144.
167. ibid. pp. 142-3.
168. Tablet revealed by 'Abdu'l-Bahá for Jakob and Anna Kunz, 30 May 1921, translated by Azizullah Khan S. Bahadur at Haifa.
169. Letter from Chris Ruhe-Schoen to the author, 7 March 1985.
170. Tablet revealed by 'Abdu'l-Bahá for Jakob and Anna Kunz, 8 October 1921, at Haifa.
171. Annamarie Honnold, 'Notes on My Mother, Anna Kunz', p. 4.
172. Joel Stebbins, 'Jakob Kunz, 1874-1938', *Popular Astronomy*, vol. 17, no. 3 (March 1939), pp. 4-5.
173. Margaret Kunz-Ruhe, 'Biography of Anna Kunz', p. 1.
174. ibid. p. 3.
175. Letter from Margaret Kunz-Ruhe to her grandchildren, undated.
176. ibid. p. 1.
177. ibid. p. 2.
178. Notes from Sylvia Paine Parmelee, 9 April 1985.
179. Margaret Kunz-Ruhe, 'Biography of Anna Kunz', p. 4.
180. Cited in a letter from Chris Ruhe-Schoen to the author, 7 March 1985.
181. Joel Stebbins, 'Jakob Kunz 1874-1938', *Popular Astronomy*, vol. 17, no. 3 (March 1939), p. 4.
182. Annamarie Honnold, 'Notes on My Mother, Anna Kunz', p. 2.
183. ibid. p. 4.
184. Margaret Kunz-Ruhe, 'Biography of Anna Kunz', p. 4.
185. Letter from Chris Ruhe-Schoen to the author, 7 March 1985.
186. Joel Stebbins, 'Jakob Kunz, 1874-1938, *Popular Astronomy*, vol. 17, no. 3 (March 1939), p. 5.
187. Cited in a letter from Chris Ruhe-Schoen to the author, 7 March 1985.

188. Cited in ibid.
189. Shoghi Effendi, *Messages to America*, p. 89.
190. Anna Kunz, 'A Bahá'í in Switzerland: Excerpts from Letters to Her Daughters', *World Order*, vol. 14, no. 12 (March 1949), pp. 401-2.
191. ibid. p. 402.
192. 'Fritzi Shaver', *Bahá'í World*, vol. 13, p. 918.
193. Letter written on behalf of Shoghi Effendi to Anna Kunz, 14 October 1947.
194. Anna Kunz, 'A Bahá'í in Switzerland: Excerpts from Letters to Her Daughters', *World Order*, vol. 14, no., 12 (March 1949), pp. 402-3.
195. ibid. pp. 405-6.
196. ibid. pp. 406-7.
197. ibid. p. 408.
198. *Bahá'í World*, vol. 12, p. 51.
199. Anna Kunz, 'A Bahá'í In Switzerland: Excerpts from Letters to Her Daughters', *World Order*, vol. 14, no 12 (March 1949).
200. Letter written on behalf of Shoghi Effendi to Anna Kunz, 21 July 1949.
201. Shoghi Effendi, *Messages to the Bahá'í World*, pp. 22-3.
202. Margaret Kunz-Ruhe, 'Biography of Anna Kunz', p. 5.
203. *Bahá'í News*, June 1953, pp. 7-10, 3-4.
204. ibid. p. 8.
205. Margaret Kunz-Ruhe, 'Biography of Anna Kunz'.
206. Words of Daniel Schaubacher at the funeral of Anna Kunz in Bern, Switzerland, translated from the German by Emer Gallagher.
207. ibid.
208. Rúḥíyyih Rabbaní, *Priceless Pearl*, pp. 134-5.
209. ibid. p. 135.
210. ibid.
211. *Bahá'í News*, July 1962, p. 9.
212. Margaret Kunz-Ruhe, 'Biography of Anna Kunz', p. 6.
213. Letter from Sylvia Paine Parmelee to the author, 9 April 1985.
214. Daniel Schaubacher, words spoken at the funeral of Anna Kunz, translated from the German by Emer Gallagher.
215. Letter from Annamarie Honnold to the author, 20 February 1985.

216. Cited in Margaret Kunz-Ruhe, 'Biography of Anna Kunz',
    p. 7.
217. ibid.
218. Cited in ibid.
219. Annamarie Honnold, *Vignettes from the Life of 'Abdu'l-Bahá*,
    p. xi.
220. Sala, 'Notes about Mrs Collins', p. 1.
221. 'Nellie Stevison French', *Bahá'í World*, vol. 12, p. 700.
222. Faizi, *Milly*, p. 2.
223. Tablet of 'Abdu'l-Bahá to Amelia Collins, 6 December 1919,
    cited in 'Amelia E. Collins', *Bahá'í World*, vol. 13, p. 834.
224. Faizi, *Milly*, p. 3.
225. 'Amelia E. Collins', *Bahá'í World*, vol. 13, p. 834.
226. Faizi, *Milly*, p. 7.
227. ibid. pp. 6-7.
228. ibid. p. 3.
229. ibid. pp. 3-4.
230. ibid. pp. 4-5.
231. Shoghi Effendi, *Bahá'í Administration*, p. 42.
232. *Star of the West*, vol. 14, no. 3, p. 75.
233. Faizi, *Milly*, p. 5.
234. ibid. p. 6.
235. 'Hómfrídur Arnadóttir', *Bahá'í World*, vol. 13, p. 943.
236. *Bahá'í News Letter*, January 1925, p. 3.
237. Faizi, *Milly*, p. 18.
238. ibid. p. 8.
239. Sala, 'Notes about Mrs Collins', p. 3.
240. ibid. p. 4.
241. ibid. p. 3.
242. Faizi, *Milly*, pp. 9-10.
243. Cited in ibid. pp. 10-11.
244. *Bahá'í World*, vol. 7, p. 59.
245. Cited in ibid. p. 61.
246. Cited in ibid.
247. Cited in Faizi, *Milly*, pp. 8-9.
248. *Bahá'í World*, vol. 7, p. 61.
249. Faizi, *Milly*, p. 9.
250. Shoghi Effendi, *Messages to America*, p. 13.
251. 'Amelia E. Collins', *Bahá'í World*, vol. 13, p. 836.
252. 'Current Bahá'í Activities', *Bahá'í World*, vol. 8, p. 102.
253. Sala, 'Notes about Mrs Collins', pp. 1-2.

254. 'May Ellis Maxwell', *Bahá'í World*, vol. 8, p. 642.
255. Rabbaní, *Priceless Pearl*, p. 155.
256. Collins, 'A Bahá'í Shrine in Latin America', *World Order*, vol. 9, no. 9, pp. 303-4.
257. ibid. p. 305.
258. ibid.
259. ibid. p. 307.
260. 'Amelia E. Collins', *Bahá'í World*, vol. 13, p. 838.
261. ibid. pp. 836-7.
262. ibid. pp. 838-9.
263. Sala, 'Notes about Mrs Collins', p. 1.
264. 'Abdu'l-Bahá, *Will and Testament*, pp. 12-13.
265. Shoghi Effendi, quoted in Rabbaní, *Priceless Pearl*, pp. 258-9.
266. 'Amelia E. Collins', *Bahá'í World*, vol. 8, p. 839.
267. ibid.
268. 'Abdu'l-Bahá, *Tablets of the Divine Plan*, pp. 32-3
269. 'Amelia E. Collins', *Bahá'í World*, vol. 8, p. 837.
270. *Bahá'í News*, March 1949, p. 6.
271. *Bahá'í News*, April 1949, p. 3.
272. Rabbaní, *Priceless Pearl*, p. 251.
273. Shoghi Effendi, *Messages to the Bahá'í World*, p. 7.
274. ibid. pp. 8-9.
275. ibid. p. 20.
276. Rabbaní, *Priceless Pearl*, p. 148.
277. ibid. p. 149.
278. Letter from Ethel Revell to O.Z. Whitehead, 18 January 1976.
279. Rabbaní, *Priceless Pearl*, p. 61.
280. Faizi, *Milly*, pp. 24-5.
281. Shoghi Effendi, *Messages to the Bahá'í World*, p. 17.
282. ibid. pp. 41-2.
283. Faizi, *Milly*, p. 28.
284. ibid.
285. *Bahá'í World*, vol. 12, p. 138.
286. ibid. p. 143.
287. Shoghi Effendi, *Messages to the Bahá'í World*, p. 46.
288. ibid. p. 47.
289. ibid. pp. 153-4.
290. ibid. p. 47.
291. ibid, p. 145.

292. ibid. p. 28.
293. ibid. p. 149.
294. Rabbaní, *Priceless Pearl*, o. 158.
295. *Bahá'í World*, vol. 12, p. 176.
296. Faizi, *Milly*, p. 25.
297. Shoghi Effendi, *Messages to the Bahá'í World*, p. 170.
298. Giachery, *Shoghi Effendi*, p. 171.
299. Faizi, *Milly*, p. 25.
300. Shoghi Effendi, *Messages to the Bahá'í World*, pp. 76-9.
301. ibid. pp. 81-2.
302. Rabbaní, *Priceless Pearl*, pp. 148-9; Faizi, *Milly*, p. 31.
303. Faizi, *Milly*, pp. 31-2.
304. ibid. pp. 111-12.
305. *Bahá'í World*, p. 840.
306. ibid. pp. 124-9.
307. ibid. p. 220.
308. ibid. p. 218.
309. ibid. 220.
310. ibid. p. 222.
311. Giachery, *Shoghi Effendi*, p. 180.
312. Rabbaní, *Priceless Pearl*, p. 449.
313. *Bahá'í World*, p. 341.
314. ibid.
315. ibid. pp. 345-6.
316. ibid. p. 840.
317. ibid. p. 329.
318. ibid.
319. ibid. p. 355.
320. ibid. pp. 739-40.
321. Faizi, *Milly*, p. 30.
322. ibid. p. 35.
323. ibid. p. 37.
324. ibid. pp. 37-8.
325. ibid. p. 38.
326. ibid.
327. ibid. p. 39.
328. *Bahá'í World*, p. 840.
329. ibid. p. 40.
330. *Bahá'í News*, February 1962, p. 2.
331. Letter from Kate Dwyer to O.Z. Whitehead, 20 September 1982.

332. Letter from Kate Dwyer to O.Z. Whitehead, 14 October 1982.
333. Faizi, *Flame of Fire*, p. 4.
334. ibid. p. 5.
335. ibid. p. 10.
336. Talk by Kate Dwyer at the National Teaching Conference, Republic of Ireland, 27 December 1980.
337. ibid.
338. Bahá'u'lláh, *Tablets*, pp. 9-10.
339. Talk by Kate Dwyer at the National Teaching Conference, Republic of Ireland, 27 December 1980.
340. ibid.
341. Shoghi Effendi, *God Passes By*, p. 138.
342. Bahá'u'lláh, *Kitáb-i-Íqán*, pp. 192-9.
343. Talk by Kate Dwyer at the National Teaching Conference, Republic of Ireland, 27 December 1980.
344. ibid.
345. Quoted in letter from Kate Dwyer to O.Z. Whitehead, 14 October 1982.
346. ibid.
347. Talk by Kate Dwyer at the National Teaching Conference, Republic of Ireland, 27 December 1980.
348. ibid.
349. Letter from Kate Dwyer to O.Z. Whitehead, 14 October 1982.
350. ibid.
351. ibid.
352. ibid.
353. ibid.
354. Talk by Kate Dwyer at the National Teaching Conference, Republic of Ireland, 27 December 1980.
355. Radio interview of Kate Dwyer by George Karko, 'New Horizons', Harcourt, Victoria, September 1982.
356. Letter from Kate Dwyer to O.Z. Whitehead, 14 October 1982.
357. Talk by Kate Dwyer at the National Teaching Conference, Republic of Ireland, 27 December 1980.
358. ibid.
359. Letter from Kate Dwyer to O.Z. Whitehead, 14 October 1982.

360. Talk by Kate Dwyer at the National Teaching Conference, Republic of Ireland, 27 December 1980.
361. Letter from Kate Dwyer to O.Z. Whitehead, 14 October 1982.
362. Talk by Kate Dwyer at the National Teaching Conference, Republic of Ireland, 27 December 1980.
363. Letter from Kate Dwyer to O.Z. Whitehead, 14 October 1982.
364. Talk by Kate Dwyer at the National Teaching Conference, Republic of Ireland, 27 December 1980.
365. ibid.
366. Bahá'í International News Service, 6 June 1981, pp. 5-6.
367. Talk by Kate Dwyer at the National Teaching Conference, Republic of Ireland, 27 December 1980.
368. ibid.
369. Bahá'í International News Service, 6 June 1981, p. 6.
370. Radio interview of Kate Dwyer, 'New Horizons', September 1981.
371. Letter from Kate Dwyer to O.Z. Whitehead, 28 March 1989.
372. Letter from Kate Dwyer to O.Z. Whitehead, 23 February 1989.
373. Bahá'u'lláh, Tablets, p. 14.
374. Brown, Memories, p. 28.
375. ibid. p. 29.
376. 'Ella M. Bailey', Bahá'í World, vol. 12, p. 685.
377. Brown, Memories, p. 11.
378. 'Ella M. Bailey', Bahá'í World, vol. 12, p. 686.
379. National Bahá'í Archives, Wilmette, Illinois. Cited in Brown, Memories, p. 29.
380. Bahá'í News, 13 July 1910, p. 13.
381. 'A Pioneer at the Golden Gate', Star of the West, vol. 13, no. 8 (November 1922), p. 205.
382. As related to Charles Cornell, quoted in 'Ella M. Bailey', Bahá'í World, vol. 12, p. 686.
383. ibid.
384. 'Ella M. Bailey', Bahá'í World, vol. 12, p. 685.
385. ibid.
386. ibid.
387. ''Abdu'l-Bahá with the Children of the Friends in Chicago', Star of the West, vol. 3, no 7 (13 July 1912), p. 6.
388. ibid. p. 7.

389. 'Ella M. Bailey', *Bahá'í World*, vol. 12, p. 686.
390. Letter from Dr Robert L. Gulick to O.Z. Whitehead, 29 April 1986.
391. ibid.
392. Quoted in 'Ella M. Bailey', *Bahá'í World*, vol. 12, pp. 685-6.
393. Letter from Bahia F. Gulick to O.Z. Whitehead, 29 April 1986.
394. 'Ella M. Bailey', *Bahá'í World*, vol. 12, p. 686.
395. Letter from Robert L. Gulick to O.Z. Whitehead, 29 April 1986.
396. 'Ella M. Bailey', *Bahá'í World*, vol. 12, p. 686.
397. *Bahá'í News*, December 1931, p. 7.
398. *Bahá'í News*, February 1932, p. 5.
399. 'Ella M. Bailey', *Bahá'í News*, vol. 12, p. 686.
400. *Bahá'í News*, June 1935, p. 13.
401. Shoghi Effendi, *Unfolding Destiny*, p. 169.
402. Shoghi Effendi, *Messages to the Bahá'í World*, p. 41.
403. Shoghi Effendi, *Citadel*, p. 109.
404. *Bahá'í World*, vol. 12, p. 124.
405. 'Ella M. Bailey', *Bahá'í World*, vol. 12, p. 686.
406. ibid.
407. ibid.
408. ibid. p. 687.
409. Letter from Dr Robert Gulick Jr to O.Z. Whitehead, 29 April, 1986.
410. 'Ella M. Bailey', *Bahá'í World*, vol. 12, p. 687.
411. Shoghi Effendi, *Citadel*, p. 161.
412. Rabbaní, *Priceless Pearl*, p. 126.
413. Letter from Bahia Gulick to O.Z. Whitehead, 29 April 1986.
414. 'Ella M. Bailey', *Bahá'í World*, vol. 12, p. 688.
415. Shoghi Effendi, *Dawn of a New Day*, p. 223.
416. 'Ella M. Bailey', *Bahá'í World*, vol. 12, p. 687.
417. Shoghi Effendi, *Citadel*, p. 165.
418. Quant, 'In the Presence of 'Abdu'l-Bahá', *Bahá'í World*, vol. 12, p. 917.
419. ibid.
420. Quant, 'Some Notes on the History of the Bahá'í Faith in Johnstown', manuscript.
421. ibid.
422. 'Abdu'l-Bahá, Tablet to Johnstown Bahá'í Assembly. Partly quoted in *Star of the West*, vol. 8, no. 19 (2 March 1918), p. 242.

423. Quant, 'Some Notes on the History of the Bahá'í Faith in Johnstown', manuscript.
424. 'Ella C. Quant', *Bahá'í World*, vol. 15, p. 506.
425. Quant, 'Some Notes on the History of the Bahá'í Faith in Johnstown', manuscript.
426. ibid.
427. ibid.
428. ibid.
429. ibid.
430. Brittingham, *The Revelation of Bahä-Ulläh*, p. 2.
431. Quant, 'Some Notes on the History of the Bahá'í Faith in Johnstown', manuscript.
432. Stockman, *Bahá'í Faith in America*, vol. 2, p. 213.
433. ibid. p. 246.
434. Quoted in ibid. p. 281.
435. Quant, 'Some Notes on the History of the Bahá'í Faith in Johnstown', manuscript.
436. *Bahá'í News*, 17 May 1910, pp. 3, 11.
437. 'Ella C. Quant', *Bahá'í World*, vol. 15, p. 506.
438. *Bahá'í News*, 5 June 1910.
439. *Star of the West*, vol. 2, no. 5 (5 June 1911), p. 4.
440. Quant, 'In the Presence of 'Abdu'l-Bahá', *Bahá'í World*, vol. 12, p. 917.
441. ibid.
442. ibid.
443. ibid. pp. 918-19.
444. ibid. p. 919.
445. ibid. p. 918.
446. ibid. p. 921.
447. ibid.
448. *Star of the West*, vol. vol. 10, no. 18 (7 February 1920), p. 332.
449. *Star of the West*, vol. 10, no. 13 (4 November 1919), pp. 250-1.
450. Quant, 'Some Notes on the History of the Bahá'í Faith in Johnstown', manuscript.
451. *Bahá'í News*, March 1941, p. 8.
452. *Bahá'í News Annual Report 1945-6*, p. 13.
453. *Bahá'í News*, July 1942, p. 4.
454. *Bahá'í News*, March 1941, p. 8.
455. *Bahá'í News*, April 1937, p. 9.

456. *Bahá'í News*, April 1938, p. 7.
457. *Bahá'í News*, November 1941, p. 6.
458. *Bahá'í News*, February 1942, pp. 9-10.
459. *Bahá'í News Annual Reports 1942-3*, p. 27.
460. *Bahá'í News*, January 1944, p. 12.
461. Quant, 'I Will Come Again', *World Order*, August 1937, pp. 178-84.
462. *World Order*, March 1943, pp. 428-9.
463. ibid. p. 429.
464. ibid.
465. *World Order*, September 1943, p. 216.
466. ibid. p. 214.
467. 'Ella C. Quant', *Bahá'í World*, vol. 15, pp. 506-7.